MONEY
is my
FRIEND

by Phil Laut

Nationally known financial consultant and seminar leader describes techniques that have increased the incomes of thousands of people in all walks of life.

Published by
Vivation Publishing Co.

ABOUT THE AUTHOR

Phil Laut is a nationally known seminar leader.
He is a graduate of the Harvard Business School and served
as controller in a major computer company.

ISBN #0-9610132-2-2
Library of Congress Card Catalogue No. 79-51206

First Printing May 1979
Second Printing August 1979
Third Printing December 1979
Fourth Printing July 1980
Fifth Printing April 1981
Sixth Printing October 1981
Seventh Printing January 1982
Eighth Printing August 1982
Ninth Printing November 1982
Tenth Printing May 1983
Eleventh Printing November 1983
Twelfth Printing April 1984
Thirteenth Printing March 1985
Fifteenth Printing June 1986
Sixteenth Printing November 1986
Seventeenth Printing May 1987
Eighteenth Printing September 1987
Nineteenth Printing May 1988
Twentieth Printing December 1988

New and Expanded Edition
First Printing May 1989
Second Printing September 1990
Third Printing October 1992
Fourth Printing October 1994

VIVATION PUBLISHING CO.
PO Box 8269
Cincinnati, OH 45208 USA

Printed in
United States of America

TABLE OF CONTENTS

Vivation® is a registered service mark and
publishing trademark of
Associated Vivation Professionals.
1-800-829-2625

iv

GUARANTEE

Satisfied customers are the most valued asset of any thriving business. If *Money Is My Friend* benefits you, please tell your friends and associates about it. If you are not satisfied with this book for any reason, you can receive a full refund from the publisher by returning it to Vivation Publising Co. within one year of purchase with your sales slip or canceled check.

ACKNOWLEDGMENTS

In this revised and expanded edition, I thank the thousands of readers who have taken the ideas in this book and started their own businesses, providing independence and self-determination for themselves, a better life for their families and employment for thousands of other people. A salute to commercial pioneers everywhere.

No one writes a book alone. Many people have freely provided me with ideas and encouragement: Leonard Orr, Lucy McDowell, Bill Chappelle, Kyle Os, Sondra Ray, Bobby Birdsall, Dick Vogel, Neil Adams, Binnie Dansby, and Jim Leonard to name a few.

People whose aid and support make this book possible:

Cover Design:	Handy Print, Cincinnati, OH
Typesetting:	Reporter Typographics, Cincinnati, OH
Printing:	Delta Lithograph, Valencia, CA
Word Processing Software:	Microsoft Corp.
Word Processing Hardware:	Zenith Data Systems
Order Fulfillment:	The Creative Source, El Toro, CA

Foreign Language Editions

CZECH Talpress Publishing U jezera 2041 155 00 Praha 5 CZECH REPUBLIC FAX: 422-651-1189	**KOREAN** Mee Too Publishing Co. 135-120 Kwanglim B/D 4F 662-14 Sinsa-dong, Kangam-ku Seoul KOREA Phone: 517-8033 FAX: 517-8035
DUTCH de Zaak de Savornin. Lohmanplein 4a 9722 HP Groningen NETHERLANDS Phone: 50-266-157 FAX: 50-252-361	**PORTUGUESE** Editoria Pensamento Rua Dr Mario Vicente 374 04270 Sao Paulo SP BRAZIL Phone: 011-272-1399 FAX: 0055-011
FRENCH Les Editions - MCL C.P. 402 - Succ. H Montreal, QUE H3G 2L1 CANADA	**SERBO-CROATIAN** Dusan Simonivic Kate Pejnovic 4 41320 Kutina YUGOSLAVIA
GERMAN Wilhelm Goldmann GmbH. PO Box 800709 D-8000 Munchen GERMANY Phone: 089-431-890	**SLOVAK** Vesna Záhradnícka 93 82108 Bratislava SLOVAKIA Phone: 653-36
HUNGARIAN Roberta Gyulainé-Nagy Köérberki út 37/D/2 H-1112 Budapest HUNGARY	**SPANISH** Kurt Denker Apartado Postal 7-1243 06700 Mexico DF MEXICO Phone: 525-761-89-29 FAX: 525-588-06-70
ITALIAN Gruppo Editoriale Muzzio Riv. Albert. Mussato 39 I-35139 Padova ITALY Phone: 049-8757 186	**SPANISH** Ediciones Obelisco Consejo de Ciento 591 08013 Barcelona SPAIN Phone: 232-7553 FAX: 447-0046

INTRODUCTION

Welcome to the adventure of building a prosperity consciousness.

What you can expect to receive from the information presented in *Money is My Friend* is:

- A thorough understanding of the FOUR LAWS of WEALTH.
- Increased Income.
- A light-hearted attitude and sense of self-reliance about your financial problems.
- The information you need to start and prosper in the career you want.

Money is My Friend will introduce you to THE FOUR LAWS OF WEALTH. These four simple laws govern all wealth and are practiced by financially successful people, stock companies and financial institutions. The practices and techniques that are discussed in *Money is My Friend* will enable you to apply the FOUR LAWS OF WEALTH to your personal finances.

The first of the FOUR LAWS OF WEALTH is the EARNING LAW.

THE EARNING LAW is

ALL HUMAN WEALTH IS CREATED BY THE HUMAN MIND.

The application of the EARNING LAW involves the pleasurable creation of a sufficient income.

THE SPENDING LAW is

THE VALUE OF MONEY IS DETERMINED BY THE BUYER AND SELLER IN EVERY TRANSACTION.

Application of the SPENDING LAW involves enjoyment of the things that you spend money for and living within your means.

THE SAVING LAW is

THE ACCUMULATION OF A SURPLUS FROM YOUR INCOME.

Application of the SAVING LAW involves saving a percentage of your income. This habit produces an attitude of extra, of abundance, which you can expect to see reflected in your future income.

THE INVESTING LAW is

SPENDING YOUR CAPITAL IN YOUR NAME FOR THE PURPOSE OF INCREASING YOUR INCOME.

Application of the INVESTING LAW is a combination of the first three LAWS OF WEALTH as the factors of earning, spending and saving all come into play. Included in the explanation of the INVESTING LAW are ideas about selling and about your own business.

Money is My Friend contains an abundance of ideas, practices and techniques to make your financial life more satisfying. Money Is My Friend has been in publication continuously since 1979. Over 100,000 copies have been sold of the English language edition alone. During this time, I have discovered that the people who have benefited the most from *Money is My Friend* have been the ones who have been willing to read it more than once. I invite you to take your time with this book. Please try out the ideas you like the best; once you have mastered a few; come back for another reading.

CHAPTER I

Prosperity Consciousness

The purpose of this book is to eliminate poverty in the world and to make abundant living socially acceptable. You can master the principles in here and use them to become wealthy. No special education or training, is required; in fact, you may discover that the training that your unconconscious mind has already received is what is holding you back. Since 1976, I have been conducting seminars and doing individual consulting with people about money. In writing this book, I have included the most valuable ideas about money that I can think of. For some readers the ideas in this book may be new or seem strange at first. Psychologists have found that as many as six repetitions of an idea are necessary before new information becomes a part of a person's consciousness. For this reason, it is a good idea to re-read this book from time to time. You will find that concepts that you missed on previous readings will flash into your consciousness as though you had never read them before. I invite you to get your money's worth. A good way to use this book is to re-read it from time to time and make a list of the practices in here that you are not now using. Pick out the one you like the best and start using it.

This book is about achieving **FINANCIAL FREEDOM**. Financial Freedom is when you never do anything that you don't want to for money and you never omit doing something that you want to do because of lack of money. Another way of describing the condition of financial freedom is that money works for you instead of you working for money. Building a **PROSPERITY CONSCIOUSNESS** is the way to ensure your

1

financial success. A prosperity consciousness is the ability to function effortlessly and conveniently in the physical world, having money or not. The progressive construction of a prosperity consciousness makes financial freedom a realistic possibility. You will find that a prosperity consciousness will produce cash for you every time as well as several other important benefits. I have observed that negative ideas about survival and dependency are the ones that tend to hold money problems in place. A prosperity consciousness not only makes it easy and fun to solve your money problems, but it will provide you emotional security and a pervasive sense of self-reliance.

If you plan to live in a society that uses money as a means of exchange, then it is intelligent to master money. People with a prosperity consciousness know that money is one of the least important things in life. If you haven't mastered money yet, the tendency is to worry about it constantly. Constant worry does little to improve your cash flow. This book is a way out of that bind.

I have purposely made this book brief. You will find that it is packed with useful money ideas. For this reason I recommend you take your time reading it and make a special note to re-read the sections that make you angry, skeptical or afraid.

CHAPTER II

The Earning Law

The progressive construction of a prosperity consciousness involves psychological and practical mastery of **THE FOUR LAWS OF WEALTH**. In this book you will be introduced to:

I. **THE EARNING LAW**
II. **THE SPENDING LAW**
III. **THE SAVING LAW**
IV. **THE INVESTING LAW**

The **EARNING LAW** is the most important. If you haven't mastered the **EARNING LAW**, then the others are just intellectual concepts.

In talking about the **EARNING LAW** I want to be very scientific. Science is concerned with determining the cause and effect of things. So we want to be very scientific here and determine the causative factor that produces wealth in every case. Once we uncover this, it will no longer be necessary for you to rely on luck or any other external factors to increase your income.

There are several popular myths that need to be dealt with on the way to uncovering THE **EARNING LAW**. These are the things that our parents, our teachers, our guidance counselors and other, wise, but perhaps not so financially successful, people have taught us about money. The most popular myth that I have identified is that hard work is the causative factor that produces wealth—that earning money is an inherently unpleasant activity. The statistics that I have read do not support this. The Social Security Administration tells me that the average cash assets of a person reaching age 65 in this country are $250. This is the richest country in the world, and these are people who worked for money 40 hours per week for 40 years or so. If working hard for money produced wealth, then it would produce wealth in every case. Rich people work a lot less than poor people do. The idea that hard work is required to be wealthy has been codified into the Puritan Work Ethic and its futility is daily demonstrated in the frustration of the middle-class American Work-aholic. If your parent(s) came home from work tired every day, then it is likely that you borrowed this myth from them. If you are working only for the money, you have probably already discovered that money is never enough reward. Those people who work only for the money have a tendency to create debts and installment payments for the things that they have bought in an attempt to give themselves the satisfaction that they miss at work.

Another common myth about money is that it is not right to enjoy yourself and get paid for it. One day I was at Boston Garden watching a Celtics game along with fifteen thousand people or so who had paid $3.50 to $8.00 to watch the game. The spectators were enjoying themselves. Then I noticed the ushers, who looked less happy, despite the fact that they were engaged in the same activity as the spectators—that is, sitting in a seat, watching the game. I thought it would be interesting to take a little poll. I sat down next to ten of the ushers, one at a time, and asked each of them the same question. "Are you enjoying the game?" I was a little surprised to discover that none of them even answered the question because they were too busy complaining to me about what a crummy job it was to be an usher. Ultimately, the only difference between the ushers and the spectators was that the ushers were being paid to be there and the spectators had paid to be there. I doubt that any of the ushers were millionaires. And most millionaires that I know enjoy their work much more than the ushers reported.

Another popular myth about money is that the right occupation is the key to financial success. This idea is frequently extolled by guidance counselors and matchbook covers— "Twelve Ways to Success—be a surveyor, a motel operator, etc." An extreme example is in the movie "The Graduate," where Dustin Hoffman hears "plastics" whispered in his ear. If you think about it for a few moments, you can probably identify people who are financially successful and people who are not, in almost every occupation. Additionally, there are people who are financially successful in some of the most improbable occupations that you can imagine. If you would like to be convinced of this, then you can sit down and read the Yellow Pages of the telephone directory someday.

Another common myth about money is that education will ensure your financial success. This idea is especially common among educators, whose great influence on students accounts for the idea having far more popularity than validity. If this were true ultimately, then college professors would be the richest people in the country. Most educators I know are poor with the exception of a few who have written successful books. One day I accompanied a friend when she was visiting the employment security office in San Francisco to pick up her unemployment check. Since I had never visited an unemployment office before, I thought it would be an interesting adventure. The lines were long and after a while I got tired of standing around, so I decided to take another poll. I went up and down the lines of people waiting for their unemployment checks and asked the same question of about fifty individuals: "What did you do for money before you were unemployed?" Almost all the answers were different. I found unemployed waitresses, accountants, factory workers, secretaries, there was even a guy there who was a marine designer with a Ph.D. in marine engineering.

Another common myth about money is that there is not enough to go around—that the more you have, the less there is for everyone else, so that it is better to be poor and righteous than rich and evil. People with this idea usually resent rich people. Ironically, it is this resentment of rich people that keeps them poor, because they would resent themselves a lot more if they became rich. The truth is that money was invented by people for their own convenience, and since your money comes from people, the only thing you can do with it is to give it to other people. This is true unless you are in the habit of stuffing your mattress with your extra greenbacks. If you spend money, you prosper other people; if you save money, you prosper others because the bank takes the money you deposit and loans it to others; and if you invest money, then you are simply giving it to someone else to spend in your name. I like what Alan Watts said about money. He asked his father how come there was a Depression. His father told him it was because they had run out of money. This seemed ridiculous to him; like a carpenter showing up for work one day and being told that he couldn't work because they had run out of inches.

Money is blamed for personal and social problems that are caused by lack of money or love of money. One of the factors that prompted me to write this book was the realization that money cannot cure poverty. It is only necessary to study the Federal anti-poverty programs of the mid 1960's to discover this for yourself. The basic idea of the anti-poverty program was that the problem with poor people was that they had no money. This leads to the erroneous conclusion that the way to solve the problem is to give poor people money. The program didn't work as intended—if it had there would be no poor people now.

There is already enough money to solve poverty several times over, and it is only practical education and banishment of erroneous thinking about money that will cure poverty.

THE EARNING LAW STATED IS THAT ALL HUMAN WEALTH IS CREATED BY THE HUMAN MIND.

This means that thought is the causative factor that creates wealth in every case. Money is composed of paper, metal and numbers—all of which are totally effect and without creative power. The key to wealth is learning how to take charge of your mind, learning how to process your mind with affirmations, studying and freeing yourself from the major inhibitors of the mind, resolving your disturbing feelings about money and learning to better use your imagination. Said most simply, increasing your wealth is a matter of increasing the quality of your thoughts—increasing the quality of your thoughts about money, increasing the quality of your thoughts about yourself and increasing the quality of your thoughts about what you do for money.

The study of thought is philosophy and the study of how thoughts affect our behavior is psychology. The next two chapters establish a base in these two subjects that will be used throughout the rest of the book.

CHAPTER III

A Short Course in Philosophy

The purpose of philosophy is to study and describe thought and to create generally applicable ideas that will enable us to increase the quality of our lives. Philosophy with any other purpose is tyrannical dogmatism. The obvious place to begin a philosophical discussion is with the physical universe, simply because it is so obvious. By the physical universe, I mean your body, your car, your dog, the tree outside and most important for the purposes of this book, your bank account.

One of the properties of the physical universe is that it does not have the power to create itself. Rocks do not create rocks, your body does not create your body. You can see this by examining a corpse. A corpse weighs the same and contains the same chemical elements of a live body—so there must be something mystical or at least invisible going on that is related to life.

Another property of the physical universe is that it is orderly. The planets proceed around the sun in the same orderly manner as electrons proceed around the nucleus of atoms. Your life is ordered by your thoughts. My friend Bobby Birdsall describes this very simply by saying that the mind is composed of two parts—the Thinker and the Prover. The Thinker thinks and the Prover proves whatever the Thinker thinks. The Prover does not care what you think; you can think whatever you want to and the Prover will prove it to be true. The job of the Prover is to keep you from going insane; because if you went around all day thinking 'People will hurt me' and you discover that everywhere you went people loved you, this would drive you nuts.

The physical universe is created out of your thoughts. Since you can think anything you want to in infinite variety and in infinite combination, it seems that your thoughts must come from somewhere that is infinite. The infinite has the property of Oneness. This means that there can only be one infinite, or it could not be infinite.

You can think of a Three Part Creative Process that starts with the infinite which is the source of your thoughts. The second element is thought and the third element is the physical universe, the result of the thought. The following diagram depicts the Creative Process and lists some of the different names that people have used for each of the three elements.

THE CREATIVE PROCESS

Flows from left to right on this diagram. The words and phrases in each column are each different ways of describing an element of the Creative Process.

The Infinite	Thought	The Physical Universe
The Source	Knowledge	The Comforter
The Force	Idea	The Holy Spirit
The Great Spirit	Concept	Your Bank Account
God	Education	Your Body
The Father	Religion	Your Car
Infinite Being	Son	Your Lover
Infinite Potential	Attitude	Your House
The Thinker	Doing	You Personal Reality
Spirit	Infinite	Having
Being	Intelligence	Infinite Manifestation

One of the characteristics of the Creative Process is that it always works. It worked last year, it works now, it will continue to work next year, it works in New York City, it works in the middle of the ocean and it works in outer space. As a student I was always interested in learning the laws of the universe. Whenever the professor would describe a scientific law, I would ask whether it worked all the time. The professor never said

10

yes, because it seems that there are exceptions to all scientific laws.

Conscious use of the Creative Process puts at your command the power of a philosophical law that always works. There are no problems that you cannot solve with the Creative Process; it puts you in charge of your life and will make you realize that since you are the Creator of your life, you can create the way you would like it. The next three principles are practical applications of the Creative Process. Once you master them, you can have anything you want in life.

THE SELF-ANALYSIS PRINCIPLE

Applying the self-analysis principle is asking yourself, what have I been thinking that has created my life the way that it is? This principle is the basis of classical psycho-analysis. Most people do not do this because they are afraid to find out what they have been thinking. Negative thoughts only create negative results as long as you think them, so it won't hurt you to find out what they are, especially after you master the next principle which enables you to change your thoughts.

THE SUGGESTION PRINCIPLE

The suggestion principle is asking yourself 'what would I like to think in order to create my life the way I would like it.' You can apply the suggestion principle in several ways; by reading, by listening, by watching, by writing and by talking. The suggestion principle enables you to increase the quality of your thoughts by reading high quality books (like this one), by listening to cassette tapes and self-improvement seminars and by writing affirmations. An affirmation is a high quality thought that you like well enough to immerse in your consciousness. Affirmations regarding the EARNING LAW.
1) I deserve to be prosperous and wealthy.
(If money makes you feel guilty because you don't feel like you deserve it, then it is difficult to increase your income, because if you did you would just feel more guilty.)
2) It is OK for me to be paid for enjoying myself.

(Struggling and engaging in unpleasant activities just for the money makes it difficult to become wealthy.)

3) My personal connection to infinite being and infinite intelligence is adequate enough to yield me a huge personal fortune.

(Your imagination is the source of your income and the infinite being and infinite intelligence is the source of the ideas that fill your imagination.)

Writing is the fastest way to incorporate these ideas into your consciousness. I suggest that you put your name in these affirmations to make them more personal and write them in all three persons. (For simplicity, affirmations in this book are in the first person. You can convert them into the other two persons yourself.) For example, I deserve to be prosperous and wealthy. (First person)

Phil, you deserve to be prosperous and wealthy. (Second person)

Phil deserves to be prosperous and wealthy. (Third person)

Leave a space at the right hand side of your paper for the response that your mind gives you to the new thought in the affirmation and write down the responses that have emotional impact. One of the characteristics of the mind is that it tends to be associative, so it is impossible to be writing "I deserve to be prosperous and wealthy" without negative ideas that you may have about money coming to your attention.

Sample affirmation exercise:

Affirmation	Response
I deserve to be prosperous and wealthy.	Oh yeah?
I deserve to be prosperous and wealthy.	Why am I doing this?
I deserve to be prosperous and wealthy.	I feel tired
I deserve to be prosperous and wealthy.	?
I deserve to be prosperous and wealthy.	I don't want to work that hard.
Phil, you deserve to be prosperous and wealthy.	Who says?
Phil, you deserve to be prosperous and wealthy.	Not yet.

Phil, you deserve to be prosperous and wealthy.	Maybe I'll try it.
Phil, you deserve to be prosperous and wealthy.	My father told me I had to work hard.
Phil, you deserve to be prosperous and wealthy.	Why not?
Phil deserves to be prosperous and wealthy.	What will my friends think?
Phil deserves to be prosperous and wealthy.	No one ever told me so before.
Phil deserves to be prosperous and wealthy.	I'm starting to believe it.

The purpose of using all three persons in affirmations is to make it easy to discover and change your negative ideas no matter where they came from—whether you thought them up yourself, whether someone else told them to you or whether someone else said them about you. It is a very good idea to breathe fully and deeply while you are writing affirmations. If you get the same response over and over, it is a good idea to invent an affirmation that is the opposite of that response. For example, if 'I don't want to work that hard' is a continuing response, then take 'I deserve to be paid for enjoying myself' as your affirmation.

THE GOALS PRINCIPLE

The goals principle is asking yourself 'what would I like to create to have what I like'. The purpose of the goals principle is to give your mind an opportunity to create for yourself. (Some people would much rather complain about what they have than ask for what they want.) Having only realistic goals is not recommended. Realistic goals are based on your view of what can happen based on what has happened in the past. Now that you are increasing the quality of your thoughts, there is no limit as to what can happen. I suggest that you make a list of goals—all the things that you would like to be, do and have. Another way to do it is to think of the different areas of your life and write down what you would like. It is a good idea to have commercial goals for your business, social goals for your relationships, psychosomatic goals for your body and intellectual goals for skills that you would like to acquire.

MONEY AND SPIRITUALITY

There have been some negative ideas floating around for a very long time that effect spiritual people as they work at building their prosperity consciousness and creating abundance in their lives. Some of these negative ideas are that money and spirituality don't mix, that the material world is an illusion, that "money is the root of all evil." These ideas are based on the old view that God and Man are separate and that it's holier to wait to experience abundance until you're there (with God in Heaven) rather than enjoy it here and now on earth. Although Western religions paid lip service to the idea that God is everywhere, the fact that God might be riding around with you in your Mercedes, and enjoying it too, was not well publicized.

The truth is that the universe is made up of Divine Substance—which is God and nothing but God. You can't get away from God by being materialistic; you are immersed in God and there's no way out. Furthermore, there is not one single particle of the physical world that is not in essence OK with God.

Having a prosperity consciousness enables you to function easily and effortlessly in the material world. The material world is God's world, and you are God being you. If you are experiencing pleasure and freedom and abundance in your life, then you are expressing your true spiritual nature. And the more spiritual you are, the more you deserve prosperity.

When the charge is gone from your experience of money, it becomes highly abstract and mystical stuff. It symbolizes both the infinite and the finite. It is the power of God on the material plane, which is the power of wealth. It allows you to materialize and dematerialize things at will, just like God. It allows you to create beauty in your life and in the lives of others. Your use of the power of wealth can be an act of faith, love and thanksgiving every instance.

Affirm your connection to Infinite Being and Infinite Intelligence often. Your consciousness of your connection to Infinite Being and Infinite Intelligence is your most valuable personal asset.

Money Affirmations

1) I deserve to be prosperous and wealthy.
2) I deserve to be paid for enjoying myself.
3) My personal connection to infinite being and infinite intelligence is adequate enough to yield me a large personal fortune.
4) Money is my friend.
5) I have plenty of money.
6) I am at one with the power that is materializing my desires.
7) My presence alone produces valuable results.
8) My financial life is easy.
9) It is OK for me to exceed my goals.
10) Beauty, power and harmony abound in my mind.
11) It is fun for me to be a wealthy (wo)man.
12) I now allow others to support my financial success.
13) My well-being has nothing to do with my financial success.
14) I forgive myself for using money to control people.
15) I forgive myself for wasting money.

RECEIPT

No. 619865

DATE 8/23/03

$8-55

FROM Janice Stafford

FOR Book - Money is My Friend

DOLLARS

○ FOR RENT
○ FOR

CASH ☒
CHECK ○
MONEY ORDER ○

FROM _____ TO _____

BY _____

ACCT.	
PAID	
DUE	

2501

CHAPTER IV

Psychology and Prosperity

Psychology is the study of how thoughts affect people's behavior. In this chapter you will learn about the effect of thought structures on prosperity, how unresolved feelings limit your income production and learn about the major inhibitors of the human mind—**THE FIVE BIGGIES.**

The thoughts that cause people the most trouble are the ones that are connected with survival and security. The tendency is to cling to even negative thoughts that you think are necessary for survival. When you sleep, you lapse into a pre-verbal state of consciousness where for the most part you do not have conscious control of your thoughts. This fact should indicate that the world is safe for you, that there are no thoughts necessary to your survival.

Another category of thoughts that cause problems are the thoughts related to getting approval or love from other people. These are related to survival because during our infantile helplessness (when thought patterns were first formed), it appeared that our survival was dependent upon the approval (or at least the sufferance) of others. Some examples of thoughts like this are:

> I have to fight for what I want.
> No one wants me.
> I am helpless and dependent.
> It is not safe to be truthful,
>   etc, etc.

The key here is to realize that you are your own source of love. It is impossible to love someone else more than you love yourself; it is impossible to experience more love from someone else than you are willing to give yourself. Another way of saying this is that once you begin to enjoy your own company, it becomes a lot easier to enjoy the company of someone else.

THE FIVE BIGGIES

In my consulting work I have found that the major inhibitors of the human mind could be classified into the Five Biggies. The Five Biggies are Birth Experience, Parental Disapproval Syndrome, Specific Negatives, Unconscious Death Urge and Other Lifetimes.

BIRTH EXPERIENCE

Birth was a confusing event that marked the end of a nine month period of relaxation in the womb. In the womb, the kundalini energy which built your body in the first place flowed uninhibitedly, all of your needs were met without your doing anything, and life had a sense of timelessness and oneness about it. Birth was your first social experience, that is the first experience you had with people that you could see. The conclusions that you made about life at birth are important to know about and to change in developing a prosperity consciousness. Almost everyone learned how to breathe after the umbilical cord was cut. This means that breathing was learned in fear and panic of death. For this reason almost everyone breathes less than fully and freely. Breath is the connection between the visible and the invisible. Breath is the connection between the God within and the God without. Breathing is the activity that we do the most of. Mastering your breath is an eminently practical thing to do whether you would like to increase your income or not. Solitude is joyous if you are breathing fully and freely. If you are not then solitude becomes loneliness and distressing because the lack of distraction allows the struggle that is required for you to breathe comes to your attention. Vivation is the technique that is receiving world-wide acceptance as a method of freeing the breath from the negative experience of birth, as well as producing resolution of suppressed feelings from any part of your life. Learning Vivation involves relaxing and breathing in the presence of a professional coach. Currently there are hundreds of Vivation Professionals offering this technique to people. For more information about Vivation, I suggest that you read Vivation—The Science of Enjoying All of Your Life by Jim Leonard and Phil Laut ISBN: 0-9610132-4-9 or phone 1-800-829-2625 for free information.

I want to suggest a simple exercise so that you can get an idea of the power of your breath. Lie down in a relaxed position and close your eyes. Take twenty even medium-speed breaths in and out through your mouth being careful to connect the inhale with the exhale and the exhale with the inhale in a continuous rhythm. Then take four long, easy breaths. Then back to the twenty medium-speed breaths as before and so on. A few minutes of this exercise will give you a hint of the pleasure you can experience in a Vivation session. The pleasure is probably more than you can imagine.

The essence of the birth experience is unexplained emotions. Said another way, it is the confusion between love and pain. This confusion manifests in people's lives with the idea that it is possible to suffer enough to earn bliss. If you think you can struggle enough to earn bliss, you are a bit like the ancient pagans who thought they could prevent earthquakes by sacrificing goats. The trouble with this way of thinking is that it produces eternal anxiety, because no one ever comes along to tell you that you have sacrificed enough goats.

As you begin to unravel significant events in your personal history—the events surrounding birth and parental conditioning, you will discover that the events are not the important things. The events, no matter how terrifying, are over and done; they are in the past. Resolving our suppressed feelings and uncovering the ideas and rules about life that we made as a result of these events is the important thing. The tendency is to keep operating on these unconscious rules until they are consciously changed.

When I started to travel around the country conducting my seminars, I was successful right from the beginning no matter where I went. However, I found that the seminars that I conducted when I was at home were poorly attended. It was

19

interesting for me to see that a teacher of prosperity principles would have his income go almost to zero whenever he went home. When I started thinking about this problem I remembered that when I was a child, my father had commuted from New Jersey to New York City to work. I thought that I was copying his example of having to travel away from home to earn an income. I started writing affirmations like, "I am not my father. It is easy for me to produce an income at home." Nothing happened. The next time I went home, my income was even less than it had been before. By this time I had had enough Rebirthing sessions that it was pretty easy for me to recall incidents from my birth and my infancy. When I started to think about this problem again, I recalled being in the nursery just after my birth. The door to the room opened and a hospital attendant walked in. I jumped in fright at the prospect of being mishandled again, until I took a second look and noticed that the attendant was about forty feet away. My next thought was, 'I don't have to worry about him, I only have to worry about the people close to me.' I knew this was related to my problem with my income, so I took the affirmation, "I am willing to trust people near me." The next time I went home, my business there started providing me with the abundance that I had previously enjoyed only on the road.

(A note for the skeptical. At my seminars normal skepticism that anyone can remember back so far is often expressed by participants who have read this book. Admittedly it is unusual to remember one's birth and infancy; but it is only unusual from a statistical point of view, because most people don't. Some people recall very little from their childhood. Clearly what you remember has nothing to do with time. Most teenagers don't recall their birth and most sixty year olds can remember being a teenager. If time were the governing factor, then, by this logic, most teenagers would recall their birth. It is natural to remember everything and effort is required to suppress memory. For this reason, remembering harder doesn't work. The events that are forgotten in your past are forgotten as the result of an unconscious decision to suppress the pain associated with them.

THE PARENTAL DISAPPROVAL SYNDROME

The essence of the parental syndrome is the idea that love is something that you get only if you earn it. Another way of saying this is that the parental disapproval syndrome is the belief in limits that can be overcome by struggle. Regarding money, it is the idea that it is necessary to perform some unpleasant task to earn money and if you are lucky, you might get to enjoy spending it. The parental disapproval syndrome is the biggest biggie regarding money. For this reason I have devoted the next chapter to exercises so that you can unravel it in your consciousness. Also the chapter after next is devoted to several cases of the parental disapproval syndrome. Children are unabashed expressions of divinity and are very loving. The close connection that children feel with their parents, especially with their mother causes them to imitate their parents. Because of their uninhibited intuitive abilities, children tend not only to imitate their parents' behavior, but also their thoughts. To most parents it is a little disconcerting to see their subconscious acted out in three dimensions. Parents react to their discomfort by providing their children with a bunch of rules about how to act—rules for right thinking, rules for the right use of time, rules about reward and punishment, all of which impose limits and act to inhibit the divinity of the child. After a while, most children give up trying to overtly get what they want outside of the rules that have been established, once they realize that it is not safe to be a rebel, at least not openly. Since it was not safe to express hostility that you felt as a child, it is probably suppressed in your consciousness, from where it operates without your awareness, and apparently without your control. It is the hostility that people feel toward their spouses, their children, their bosses, the government and so forth. The value of understanding the parental disapproval syndrome in your consciousness is that it is much easier to resolve the hostility once you understand its source. It is a good idea to

21

close your eyes and imagine your parents as small children. This will give you the opportunity to tell them what you always wanted to in a safe way. I am only being a little facetious when I say that in order to be a millionaire, all you have to do is learn how to love your parents. This means loving them because you want to and because you appreciate them, not because they told you that is what you ought to do.

SPECIFIC NEGATIVES

Specific negatives are the favorite negative ideas that people use to limit themselves. Whenever you feel depressed, write down all of your thoughts. This will transfer your depression from subjective reality to objective reality and make it easy for you to see the cause of your depression. After writing down your thoughts for fifteen minutes or so, you will probably say to yourself, 'No wonder I am depressed, anyone with thoughts like that would feel depressed.' The next step is to take the negative thoughts you were just thinking as indicated on the paper and invert them into affirmations and then write the affirmations. I have found that this simple little exercise cures depression every time.

UNCONSCIOUS DEATH URGE

Just as a person's ideas about money are the cause of his experience of money, so are a person's ideas about death the cause of his experience about death. Many of us have been trained to believe in the inevitability of death. This training frequently results in an entire belief system about death. With the idea of life extension, rejuvenation and immortalist philosophy becoming more popular, this belief system can be challenged. The unconscious death urge is the name of the belief system about death. It is based on scarcity, lack and limitation. Freeing yourself from its influence will increase your prosperity to no end.

The essence of the unconscious death urge is the helplessness and hopelessness surrounding the idea that you can't even earn the love that you want. When I first heard about immortalist philosophy, I thought it was a unique idea. I found that after one exposure to the idea that I thought about it a lot and noticed its practical aspects. I realized that the belief in the inevitability of death was a statement that the universe is a hostile place—that there is something waiting to kill you without your permission. If you have this idea, then the intelligent thing to do is to protect yourself from death. The constant effort required to protect yourself causes tension in your body. If you think that death is inevitable, then don't be surprised if people are hostile to you. Religion has never adequately explained the inevitability of death. Maybe it is just the belief in the inevitability of death that causes death to occur. In any case, you have nothing to lose by affirming your right and ability to live forever. The peace and certainty of life that will begin to inhabit your consciousness will make it easier to increase your income or anything else you want to do.

I have worked with clients whose death urges were active during the time we worked together. Just the idea of immortalist philosophy enabled them to double their incomes, because it freed their minds from the worrying that they had been doing about death. Mastering physical immortality seems to be a three-part process.

1) Master immortalist philosophy. (There are a couple of books mentioned in the bibliography to get you started.)
2) Free yourself from your own personal death urge, by rooting out any loyalty to death that still inhabits your consciousness.
3) Practical mastery of your body.

OTHER LIFETIMES

Other lifetimes are highly overrated as causative factors in this lifetime. Among the thousands of people that I have worked with, I only have encountered very few people for whom another lifetime was the major psychological causative factor in this lifetime. For this reason, I am willing to consider their importance. The parental disapproval syndrome is the biggest biggy, however, and I have noticed that the people who are very intent on blaming karma for their problems are the same ones who think it is imperative to love their parents.

23

This makes them much more willing to blame karma than their parents.

Freeing your mind from the effect of THE FIVE BIGGIES will increase your wealth, love, happiness, and health.

THE TRUTH ABOUT EMOTIONS

The truth about emotions is that bliss is your natural emotional state. Negative emotions only possess the power that you give them. You give them this power by clinging to them. The tendency to cling to them is based on the belief that they are necessary for your survival or necessary for you to get love, as described at the beginning of this chapter.

Emotions are bodily reaction to thoughts we are afraid to know about. Emotions appear to be the context within which thoughts are held; this is an illusion, however, caused by the momentary power of the emotion, which blocks your mind from seeing the thought that caused the emotion in the first place. When you are willing to relax into your emotions, that is sink in to them instead of running away, it becomes easy to see the thoughts that cause them.

Your natural state as a powerful, intelligent being is bliss. Bliss is a pervasive feeling of well-being for no apparent reason. Other descriptions of this feeling are peace, joy, acceptance, calm, relaxation, samadhi, love, power—all of which result in feeling loving. Negative emotions occasion feeling unloving. The prevalent thought accompanying a negative emotion is the thought of being helpless to change it. In fact, it is the struggle to control or change your emotions that keeps the negative emotion in place. The following table is designed to give you a clear understanding of negative emotions and make it easy to free yourself from them.

Negative Emotion	Definition
Anger	Intention contaminated with the idea of helplessness.
Rage	Extreme anger.
Resentment	Long standing anger.
Fear	Contemplation of some future change that you don't like and which you can do nothing about
Sadness	Rage at being attached.
Grief	Extreme sadness. Rage with regard to loss.
Jealousy	Present time fear of future time loss. This usually involves seeing someone else have the fun that you are not willing to allow yourself.
Guilt	Fear of punishment, usually resulting in self-punishment before someone else can do it.
Pride	Temporary feeling of well-being, at the expense of another.
Apathy	Rage turned against yourself in the form of self-hate
Admiration	The highest form of apathy. Admiration is inactive. You can admire someone forever and it will never do you a bit of good.
Lust	Exaggerated alienation—a form of resentment bringing past losses into the present.
Greed	Lust with regard to money.
Gluttony	Lust with regard to food.
Smoking	Lust with regard to breathing.

Remedy	Sample Affirmations
Forgiveness	I forgive my parents and doctor for the pain they caused me at birth. I acknowledge their love for me and mine for them. I forgive myself for not receiving what I wanted.
Safety	As long as I breathe, my body is safe. Fear is safe for me. The margin of safety increases in my environment every day.
Free the other person or thing from your need.	I am a self-determined person and I allow others the same right
Self-reliance	The more freedom I allow others, the more freedom there is for me. The less I need others, the easier it is for them to love me.
Self-forgiveness	I am innocent. I am a child of God. All my desires are holy and they always have been.
Let go of your desire to prove something.	It is easy for people to see how wonderful I am. I now feel comfortable in the presence of everyone.
Self-love	I like myself. I am a lovable person. I no longer have to earn money and love. I am lovable and capable.
Remind yourself that you deserve it.	I deserve to be prosperous and wealthy. I deserve love whether I am successful or not.

More Affirmations

BIRTH
1. I forgive my parents and doctor for the pain they caused me at birth. I acknowledge their love for me and mine for them.
2. I survived my birth. I have the right to be here.
3. I am glad I was born and so is everyone else.
4. I am now breathing fully and freely.
5. I no longer fear irreparable damage.
6. I now feel loved and connected with my parents, my friends and everyone who is important to me.

RELATIONSHIPS
1. I am no longer afraid of my parents' disapproval.
2. I am no longer afraid of my father's disapproval.
3. I am no longer afraid of my mother's disapproval.
4. Disapproval is OK with me.
5. I receive assistance and co-operation from those people everywhere necessary to achieve my desired result.
6. Everything works out more exquisitely than I plan it.
7. I am willing to allow more bliss, love and money into my life than I could imagine before.
8. I am now willing to succeed.

ALIVENESS
1. My infinite life stream has the ability to heal every cell in my body.
2. Since I am the person who knows the most about my body, it is easy for me to heal it.
3. I can live forever on bacon and eggs and chocolate cream pie.
4. My wealth contributes to my aliveness and to the aliveness of others.
5. I am at cause over money.
6. I am at cause over my body.

CREATIVE SELF-IMAGE

1. I, (your name) , like myself. I am a lovable person.
2. I am now highly pleasing to myself.
3. I am highly pleasing to myself in the presence of others.
4. I am highly pleasing to others and others are highly pleasing to me.
5. I am a self-determined person and I allow others the same right.
6. I have a right to say NO to people without losing their love.
7. Other people have the right to say NO to me without hurting me.
8. I like myself, therefore I like others.
9. I like myself, therefore others like me.
10. I like others, therefore others like me.
11. I like others, therefore others like themselves.
12. The more I like myself, the more others like themselves.

FOR SUPPRESSED HOSTILITY

1. I forgive my parents and others for their ignorant behavior toward me.
2. I forgive myself for my ignorant reactions toward them.
3. I forgive myself for hating my parents and other people.
4. I forgive others for hating me.
5. I forgive myself for not hating my parents and other people when it was appropriate, or when they deserved it.
6. I'm glad other people don't always express their hostility towards me when I think I deserve it.
7. I now feel loved and appreciated by my parents, my friends and everyone who is important to me.
8. I have the right and the ability to express my hostility without losing people's love, and I take responsibility to clean up the mess and restore harmony when appropriate.
9. I no longer have to be a nice guy to succeed with people.
10. I now forgive the ignorance of my doctor and parents for the pain they caused me at birth.

11. I'm glad to be out of the womb so that I can express myself fully and freely.

GENERAL ALIVENESS ENRICHMENT

1. My mind is centered in infinite intelligence that knows my good; I am one with the creative power that is materializing all my desires.
2. All the cells of my body are daily bathed in the perfection of my divine being.
3. I have enough time, energy, wisdom and money to accomplish all my desires.
4. I am always in the right place at the right time, successfully engaged in the right activity.
5. I am alive now; therefore my life urges are stronger than my death urges. As long as I continue to strengthen my life urges and weaken my death urges, I will continue to live in increasing health and youthfulness.
6. Life is eternal, and I am life. My mind as the thinking quality of life is also eternal; therefore my living flesh has a natural built-in tendency to live forever in perfect health and youthfulness.
7. My physical body is a safe and pleasurable place for me to be. The entire universe exists for the purpose of supporting my physical body and providing a pleasurableplace for me to express myself through it.
8. I now receive assistance and co-operation from people.
9. My days and nights are filled with physical and mental pleasures.
10. I now give and receive love fully.
11. The more I win, the better I feel about letting others win. The better I feel about letting others win, the more I win; therefore I win all the time.
12. I daily make valuable contributions to the aliveness of myself, to others and to humanity.

13. I no longer have to ask permission to do the things that I know should be done.

WHY YOU CAN'T BE A MILLIONAIRE UNLESS YOU ARE WILLING TO FEEL YOUR FEELINGS ABOUT MONEY

Money is a far more emotional topic than most people acknowledge. Emotions about it are commonly suppressed. My purpose in this section is to point out some of the emotions that you may have suppressed about it and to thereby aid you in realizing that there is nothing wrong or abnormal about you for having them. The biggest problem with emotions is not the emotions themselves, but rather the fact that people make themselves wrong for having uncomfortable emotions and allow themselves to be shamed about them. Your feelings and emotions are not verdicts about you. In other words, they don't mean anything, except what you think they mean. In English, we say "I am angry"; as though that statement were a complete description of us at that moment. Emotions are far less permanent and definitive than the description would indicate. They are more like internal weather. They arise un-invited and by surprise and change into something else as quickly as we are willing to accept them. Whatever the emotion MEANS about you is something that you decide. You can use any emotion to gain greater awareness and compassion of yourself or to insult and shame yourself.

Money does not seem like it should be an emotional issue. Money is expressed with numbers and numbers are subject to logical process; they can even be added, subtracted, multiplied and divided, responding to universal rules about arithmetic. I have been conducting weekend seminars in all parts of the world for many years now and have noticed that the seminar participants almost always find topics about money to be more emotionally activating than topics about sex.

Madison Avenue wants us to think that money is a solution to our problems. Or at least that the things that money will buy, that are offered by the advertisers are the solution to our problems. Perhaps for this reason, emotions about money go unrecognized.

As mentioned earlier, the problem with the emotions are not the emotions themselves, but rather how we relate to them. When we have emotions that shame us, there is a tendency to engage in some behavior to avoid feeling like that or to delude ourselves about what we are feeling by denying that it exists. Avoidance and denial are really the problems then; not the emotions themselves.

A spendthrift, for example, compulsively spends money on things he cannot afford (and really doesn't want) in order to avoid the feelings of inadequacy that are the cause of the belief that he will be OK if he just buys something. The compulsion of overspending would not last for very long unless it were denied. By acknowledging the compulsion and the problems that it creates, the spendthrift could change his habits. However, the compulsion continues in place because the spendthrift denies that it exists or denies that it causes a problem.

The person who hates his work and who is just working for the money tends to use his position or the money that he is receiving as verification of his worth, thereby avoiding the feelings of inadequacy which he needs the money to avoid, and at the same time denies his dislike for his work, by refusing to consider other options.

Clearly, you may become a millionaire by over-working and over-stressing yourself, with a single-minded drive for money at any cost (some of you may know people like this); however, these people do not FEEL like millionaires.

From an early age, we are encouraged to feel shame about having feelings,
"Don't cry!"
"Be quiet!"
"Don't be a scaredy cat!"
"Don't talk back!"
are common and frequent parental messages.

The purpose of the next section is to describe financial problems caused by unacknowledged feelings, primarily fear and shame, which can limit our success. Fear can best be

32

defined as the emotion that we experience when our mind contemplates some CHANGE in the future that we do not like. For some people, fear is more generalized than this, and they tend to experience fear when contemplating any change, even changes for the better (this could be called fear of the unknown). Shame can best be defined as the belief that you are wrong; not wrong in the sense that you just made a math error, but wrong in the sense that there is something wrong with you. The idea that there is something wrong with us is re-enforced by parental messages, religious messages and any-one who attempts to blame us for causing his problems.

Denying your feelings can be very expensive in your own business and compulsively avoiding them may prevent you from ever getting started. When you read over the next section describing the feelings that cause us problems, surely you'll see many of them that you do not like. There are probably none that you like well enough that you would wait on line to get more of them. However, feeling them will not kill you. Avoiding them or denying them can contribute to having less money than you deserve or staying at work you don't like.

Some of the feelings that cause problems in starting and succeeding in your own business are: fear of failure, fear of success, fear of rejection, fear of death, fear of the unknown, fear of change, fear of loss, shame about wanting money and shame about money in general.

FEAR OF FAILURE

If you compulsively avoid experiencing your fear of failure, it is likely that you will never even get started in your own business where failure is more evident and more possible than in a job where you can confine your activities to what you already know how to do and where the results of your efforts are clouded by the involvement of other people. If you deny that you have any fear of failure, then you are likely to make rash decisions, which you would not have made if you had been more willing to acknowledge your fear of failure and more willing to heed what your feelings were telling you, instead of trying to prove your courage.

FEAR OF SUCCESS

Fear of success is often more suppressed than fear of failure. If you now have your own business, you have already accommodated yourself to fear of failure somehow, or you couldn't keep going. Since fear of success is usually more suppressed than fear of failure; envy, resentment or jealousy regarding people more successful than you may be the only indicators of fear of success that you experience. If you compulsively avoid experiencing your fear of success, then you will tend to accept as unexamined Truth the excuses and reasons that your mind gives you to explain why you don't have what you want and you will find it impossible to take the moves and decisions that would get you what you want. If you deny that you have any fear of success, it is difficult to plan for success. The realization that success brings with it new and different problems (although success solves some problems) is often missed by those who deny that they have any fear of success.

FEAR OF REJECTION

If you compulsively avoid feeling your fear of rejection, then you will never learn to sell, because you'll never make enough sales calls to gain the experience required. Everyone is nervous when they are selling. I have had my own business for years and selling still makes me nervous. The question is not whether you are nervous; but rather whether you choose to allow your desire to suppress the nervousness to prevent you from having the success that you want. If you deny that you have any fear of rejection, then it is likely that you will accept some other reason that your mind offers you about why you are unwilling to sell.

FEAR OF DEATH

Fear of death is strongly associated with issues about money and success. The language that we use is a clue to this — "earn a living", "a living wage", "work yourself to death", or "money to live on". In the strictest sense, you do not need money to live, although it is likely that you require a cash

34

flow to continue to live in your current manner. The loss of money will not necessarily contribute to or cause your death. If you think that money is essential to your survival, then you'll do anything to get it, including staying at a job that you don't want. Money is a game. The game will be a lot more enjoyable for you and you will be empowered to serve more people with your income producing activities by realizing that your survival is not at stake.

FEAR OF THE UNKNOWN

Fear of the unknown is a close companion to fear of change. Any situation that exists now, at least you know about, and any other situation will be different and therefore unknown. If you compulsively avoid experiencing your fear of the unknown then you will never make any changes in your life. Life can get pretty dull this way. If you deny that you have any fear of the unknown, then you will find it difficult to plan ahead to solve future problems before they become critical, because the planning process is activating to fear of the unknown.

FEAR OF LOSS

Sometimes in your own business, you invest your best ideas, a great deal of time, money and energy into a project that means a lot to you and you lose money. Even on successful projects in your own business, the risk of loss exists. So, if you wish to compulsively avoid fear of loss, than you'd best stay in a job where the financial risks are less obvious than in your own business. If you deny that you have any fear of loss, it is likely that you will take increasingly more foolish risks to keep convincing yourself of your courage.

SHAME ABOUT WANTING MONEY

In some people, the desire for money is subject to thinking so perverse and destructive that it is startling that they have any cash flow at all. The perverse and destructive logic goes something like this: "If I want money, it must be because I don't have enough; if I don't have enough, then that must be because I am not good enough or because what I have to offer is not good enough." At about this point in the thinking process, experiencing any desire for money becomes sufficiently uncomfortable to motivate the person to think about anything else, to end the discomfort, thereby giving up on his dreams.

For many years, at the start of the Money Seminars that I conducted, I would hold a $50 bill in front of me at arm's length, unfolded so that the audience could readily identify what I was holding. Then I would ask, "Who wants money?" Invariably less than 10% of the participants raised hands or indicated their desire for money verbally. Remember now that the people in the audience had just paid their hard earned money to learn how to make more money. "I am surprised that you are here if you don't want money", I would say, and then with greater emphasis, "Who wants money?" At this point a few more hands would go up. I continued this until someone gained the required initiative to come up to the front of the room and take the $50 bill. Incidentally, 90% of the time the person who took the money was female.

It is fine to desire money. It is OK with me for you to desire money. I doubt you'd be reading this book if you didn't. Judging from human behavior, the desire for money, or for at least what it will buy is almost universal. Whether or not this desire is acceptable, varies greatly among individuals.

Being motivated in your work SOLELY by money provides no satisfaction whatever. Find work that you love, sell yourself vigorously, deliver quality service and ask fair prices. When shame about your desire for money comes to your awareness, as it will from time to time, I suggest that you conclude that it means nothing about you and that its purpose is to remind you to treat the people who pay you whether customers or employer ethically.

SHAME ABOUT MONEY

Money is a topic that activates shame for everyone. People are ashamed they have so little or so much and are ashamed that others have so little or so much. When you are ashamed about money, no amount seems right. As described earlier, money is a whole lot more subjective and emotional than is commonly believed. Most people SAY that they want to earn more money, fewer do something about it, preferring to cling to the fantasy that things would be better, if they just had more money.

If you were to double your income every month for many months in a row as a result of effective use of the techniques in this book (or any other techniques), I doubt that you would receive notification from your bank or anyone else letting you know that you are rich. The shopper with $500 to spend at Woolworth's is likely to feel rich; the same shopper at a Rolls Royce dealer does not. James Michener in his novel "Texas" presented precise categories for gradations of wealth.

$1 to $20 million	Comfortable
$20 to $50 million	Well-to-do
$50-$500 million	Rich
$500 million-$1 billion	Big rich
$1-$5 billion	Texas rich

Whatever amount of money you have now, you will find it easier to have more, if you accept what you have as OK rather than feel ashamed about it. Money works like this: you have some and everyone else has all the rest. Unless you are the richest or poorest person in the world, there will always be people who have more money than you do and others who have less. Your ability to feel comfortable with this reality does a lot to determine your peace of mind about money. Shame about money will come to your awareness from time to time. This is fine. Use this shame to your benefit. If you are working just for a paycheck, the shame could serve as a reminder that you would better enjoy work that you love; if you have been dishonest in your dealings, the shame can serve as a reminder to shape up; if none of these are the case, it is possible that the shame has primal causes unrelated to your behavior. Money represents freedom and not being controlled by our parents and substitute authority figures. All successful people that I have discussed it with told me that they experienced some shame about money.

One of the most financially successful men I met was General Georges Doriot. He had been a General in the Army during World War II, a professor at Harvard Business School and head of AR & D, the venture capital company that invested $70,000 in the start up of Digital Equipment Corporation and sold its interest in the 1970's for $300 million. General Doriot is quoted as saying, "A man is never so naked as when he stands before his accountant." It seems to me that if a triple digit millionaire can have a bit of shame about money, it must be OK for the rest of us, too.

ACCESS TO YOUR FEELINGS

Access to your feelings about money can serve you greatly in your own business not only by enabling you to avoid the problems described above but also in making better business decisions. Especially when your business is starting and growing, your subjective awareness about the risks inherent in any action is far more important than the results of the best available financial analysis. Big mistakes at the beginning can put you out of business. Even the most sophisticated financial analysis cannot consider every relevant factor and thus serves poorly in assessing risk. In a large company where any one project has a minimal effect on the survival of the business, financial analysis is much more valuable for choosing the best projects and avoiding low return ventures. When you start your own business, it is small at first with limited human and financial resources. For this reason the willingness to experience your fears associated with your business is essential to succeed and grow.

YOUR PURPOSE IN LIFE

Without purpose, a person would have no motivation whatever. An individual's life is an expression of his purpose and goals whether these are consciously or unconsciously chosen. To clearly define your purpose:

1. Make a list of 10 or 20 personality characteristics that you like about yourself, e.g. my sense of humor, my determination, my love for my family, my desire to serve.
2. Select your four or five favorite personality characteristics.
3. Referring to these four or five favorites from #2, make a list of 10 or 20 ways that you enjoy expressing these characteristics, e.g. writing, talking, taking my children on outings.

4. From the list that you made in step 3, pick your four or five favorites.

5. Write a brief statement (25 words or less of your vision of an ideal world). Write this vision in the present tense, and in terms of how you want it to be, rather than how you want it not to be and state it .

6. Put this all together into a complete sentence in the following format. The purpose of my life is to use my (insert here your favorite items from part 2) by (Insert here your favorite items from part 4) so that insert here your vision of an ideal world.

Sample completed statement of purpose:

The purpose of my life is to use my clear self-expression, my courage, my sense of humor, my curiosity, my love of freedom by teaching, writing, travelling, learning and researching human thinking and behavior so that everyone is empowered to be, do and have what they most want.

It is possible that several iterations will be required before you have a statement of purpose that you like well enough to write on a slip of paper and carry around with you.

Some of the benefits that you can expect are that thinking and behavior that do not support your purpose will be more evident to you, and goal setting and decision making will both be easier.

The statement and expression of your purpose is derived from your values. For this reason, the clear definition of your purpose may require some careful thought to resolve conflicting values. A clear statement of purpose aids in defining goals and making decisions because it is very unlikely that a goal or decision that is not in alignment with values that matter to you can be enjoyable to accomplish or can contribute to your peace of mind. Without a clear sense of your purpose, all of the education you receive and all of the improvements that you make in yourself, serve only to make you a more productive slave to someone else's purpose.

ADDITIONAL APPLICATIONS

Many people have used this process to define the Purpose of their Love Life, the Purpose of their Business, the Purpose of their Marriage.

CHAPTER V

Increasing Your Income

Increasing your income is a matter of using your imagination in a practical and pleasurable way. Almost none of the training we received at school was in the use of creative imagination, because schools taught us to be analytical; which is to observe something that someone else created and describe its causes and effects in detail. In this chapter there are several exercises that you can do to stimulate your imagination. Many people are unaccustomed to thinking creatively, so it is likely that you'll discover that the exercises will become easier with a little practice. It is a good idea to pick an exercise that you like and do it once per day for a week in order to get the maximum value from it.

THE PERFECT CAREER FOR YOU

1. Take two minutes and write down your ten favorite pleasures.
2. Review the list and select the very favorite pleasure that you are willing to receive money for.
3. Take two minutes and make a list of ten ways that you can provide a service for people by performing your favorite pleasure that you are willing to receive money for.
4. Review the second list and pick out your favorite way of providing a service for people. What you have before you is your favorite money making idea.
5. Take another two minutes to make a list of ten things that you are willing to do to make your favorite money making idea into a financial success.
6. **THE ACID TEST** Now that you have an idea of what you can do to make your favorite money making idea a financial

success, ask yourself if you are willing to stick with it, no matter what it takes, until you receive your first $100 from it. If you are not willing to do this, then you certainly don't yet have an idea that you like well enough to succeed with. If your answer to the acid test is no, go back to step 1 and do the exercise again.

Frequently people switch jobs or careers because they feel like they have failed. If you make a habit of only devoting yourself to ideas that you like so well that you are willing to stick with them until you receive your first $100, you will never feel like you failed again. After receiving your first $100, you can decide whether you want to continue with the idea—but you will be making the choice from the position of success.

7. If the answer to the acid test is yes, simply take the list that you made in step 5 and make it into a personal calendar or schedule for yourself and start doing the things on the list.

CREATIVE SOLUTIONS TO FINANCIAL PROBLEMS

When faced with a financial problem, a common tendency is to get out your checkbook and your calculator and feverishly begin to add numbers. *It is impossible to solve financial problems with money.* Your imagination has the solution to all of your financial problems and if you want it to give you creative solutions, then you must ask it creative questions. The exercise that will bring solutions to your financial problems every time is:

Sit down and make a list headed, "Ten ways I can produce an extra $_____ before _____." The amount of money and the date you use are up to you, as you become more familiar with the exercise, it will be easy to increase the amount of money and to shorten the time. It is common for people to start with, "Ten ways I can produce an extra $15 by the end of next week."

HOW TO MAXIMIZE YOUR INCOME WORKING FOR A COMPANY OR OTHER INSTITUTION

The way to maximize your income working for someone else is to assume that you own the place and from that position do whatever it is that needs to be done. To do this, you must realize that job descriptions even when formally written are not exclusive. What I mean by this is that I never read a job description that included the phrase "and that is all." Make a list entitled "Ten things I would like to do to have this place run more smoothly." It is OK to tell people what you are doing, but it is by no means necessary. Do not worry about being compensated for the extra service that you are providing; because you are building personal certainty about your ability to make a contribution. Once you have this certainty, you can turn it into cash any time you want to, whether you are compensated for it in your present job or not. Remember, the company that you work for is your company. If you work for IBM, then IBM is your company—for sure it is the only company that you have.

NEGOTIATING A RAISE

For some people, having a job is an emotional extension of infancy, where we developed the idea that the good things in life come from one person, Mommy. You are as dependent on your job as you were on Mommy as an infant if contemplating the loss of your job puts you into a state of panic. Even suppressed panic about losing your job reduces your creativity and effectiveness that you could be using to advance yourself. Begin a savings plan immediately to reduce your dependence on your job. By saving the first 10% of your income and leaving the interest to accumulate, you can have 6 months income in about four years and three months income in a little more than two years. The sense of well being that you gain from having money in the bank will contribute greatly to increasing your income. I suggest that you use the principles in this book to develop other sources of income besides your job, thereby reducing dependency on your pay check.

Make a practice of negotiating your pay raises in advance instead of just accepting what you get. Now is the time to discuss next year's raise with your boss, because when you are informed about it is usually too late to change anything. Early discussion about your raise will provide you with valuable information about your employer's expectations about your performance. Learn as much as you can about your company. No matter what your job, you can probably figure ways to make improvements. When you increase your productivity, you deserve to receive a portion of the benefit that you created for your company in the form of a salary increase. Even in a well run company, the steps to take to cause things to run more smoothly and the steps to increase profits are usually quite evident with a little study. Additionally, the people who manage a well run company are often open to suggestions for improvement while those who mange poorly run companies may be defensive about suggestions and require more persuasion. Some companies pay outside consultants hundreds of dollars per hour to analyze their problems. A portion of the time that consultants are paid for is spent simply for them to learn about your company. Since you already know about your company, you are a far more economical consultant.

No matter what your job, think up ways to improve your company and negotiate a raise in advance to be paid based on your performance. In other words, learn how to sell yourself. Negotiate like this—"When I complete this project that will save the company $100,000 per year, I'd like a 20% raise. Is that agreeable?" or "I can process 500 expense vouchers per week without error instead of 300. Once I have done it, I'd like a 15% pay increase. OK?" It is possible that your employer is unaccustomed to discussions like this. Nevertheless, it is worth the effort to get started because the alternatives are either to take what you get or to change jobs in hope of getting something better.

It is important to point out that many of these ideas about increasing your income at a job may challenge long held and infrequently questioned belief systems (fantasies) about reward and recognition.

Fantasy: If I do good work, surely I will receive greater income.

Reality: The rewards from your work come from within you (the satisfaction you gain from it) and from outside you (pay and recognition). The pay and recognition that you are offered is beyond your control, and is determined by your superiors who are rewarded, in part, by their superiors for their ability to manage their expenses carefully. This means that unless you speak up for yourself before raise time, then you are allowing your salary to be determined by what you are willing to accept instead of by what you want.

Fantasy: The most effective, productive and deserving people rise to the top.

Reality: Wake up! Look around your organization or any other. Your parents may have convinced you that life is fair, or perhaps that it SHOULD be fair. Regardless of your current view about fairness, the important point is that there is no GUARANTEE of fairness. It is fine to expect to be treated fairly; but you had best learn how to speak up for yourself. Other people's ideas of fairness may be very different from yours, and you'll find out too late if you avoid discussing it.

If you refuse to grow up and free yourself from your childhood dreams about how things should be and accept the responsibility for advancing yourself, it is unlikely that anyone else will do it.

SELF-EMPLOYMENT

The reason that so few people are self-employed is that their parents told them never to do anything without instructions or permission. Employees frequently set up their employers as parent substitutes and experience the same dependency relationship with their employers that they had with their parents; and feel the resentment towards their employer that results in all dependency relationships. Sometimes I am amazed that business works as well as it does.

Ultimately the only difference between self-employment and working for someone else is that the self-employed person sells his services to many customers. The principles in the previous section are designed to enable you to adopt a self-employment mentality whether you are self-employed or not.

Most self-employed people work harder and longer than company-employed people. In fact, if most self-employed people went down to the local phone company to apply for a job and were told that they would have to work as hard as they do for themselves, they would leave quickly in search of a less demanding employer. The greatest joy of self-employment is the ability to establish your own work schedule. If you are self-employed, you will find that an hour per week sitting under a tree or taking a walk will do more for your income than working an extra two hours. This is because creative ideas spring to your awareness most easily when your mind and body are relaxed. My best ideas occur on long walks.

UNEMPLOYMENT

The purpose of unemployment and welfare benefits is to provide people a cash flow while they take the time to increase their self-esteem enough to pleasurably create a new cash flow. Regrettably, most welfare recipients and most welfare employees are not aware of this purpose. The participants in the welfare game usually resent each other and most recipients are so angry about being on welfare that they spend the checks as fast as they receive them, which tends to keep them on welfare. I have received letters from welfare mothers with five children and an estranged husband who have successfully used the principles described in this book to start their own business and end their dependency on welfare. Welfare is a wonderful invention. Since welfare was invented we have not had a severe economic depression. Welfare was probably invented by the rich. During the 1930's the rich people realized that when the poor people had no income, it was impossible for them to purchase the goods produced by the rich; so the rich people didn't have an income either. The welfare system makes it possible for the economy to keep going regardless of the economic conditions. The sooner everyone realizes this, the sooner welfare will be unnecessary.

STARTING OVER

Fear of starting over can keep you poor and dissatisfied as well. Rarely do I meet someone who has continuously engaged in the same occupation since birth; therefore everyone has already demonstrated the ability to start over. Mastering something and going on to something else is a natural tendency of

46

successful persons. If you master the **PERFECT CAREER FOR YOU** exercise at the beginning of this chapter, you can create a new job for yourself every day if you want, and be financially successful, too.

Do not wait until you are ready to start a new career. This is like standing on the edge of the high diving board waiting for it to feel right before you jump off. Let's face it, jumping off high diving boards is scary, even after you have done it a few times.

LAZINESS LEADS TO SELF-ESTEEM LEADS TO RICHES

Mastering laziness with self-esteem is an important factor in increasing your income. You can practice this by staying in bed for a whole day on regular intervals until you can do it without feeling ashamed of yourself. It is interesting to observe that the only time that most people will allow themselves the simple pleasure of relaxing in bed all day is when they are sick. Willingness to give yourself this pleasure when you are well, can cause you to be sick a lot less often. I found that it took me several attempts to master this practice, because at around 4 P.M., as I was lying there, my mind would become full of all the things I should be doing and I would find myself downstairs doing them. The first time I had stayed in bed for a whole day I was surprised to wake up the next morning and see that the world still worked; the garbage had been collected, people were going to work and children were going to school—all of this still happened without my attention. This took a big load off my shoulders.

Since the essence of the Parental Disapproval Syndrome is the idea that love is something you must earn, loving yourself while you are doing nothing is the ultimate practice of self-esteem.

SELF-ESTEEM

Self-esteem is the result of the relationship that you have with yourself. Another way of saying this is that self-esteem is the thoughts and attitudes that you have about yourself.

47

Commonly, self-esteem was randomly formed during childhood and has received little attention since. You are the person that you spend the most time with. It is impossible to love someone else more than you love yourself and it is impossible to accept more love from someone else than you are willing to receive from yourself. One time a woman stood up in one of my seminars and it was very clear that she had received the full impact of my comments about self-esteem when she said, "You know, the only problem with going on vacation is that I have to take myself along." Whether it is your desire to increase your income, to have better relationships, to master your body or whatever, the value of increasing your self-esteem cannot be over-estimated. Money will not add to your self-esteem, it works the other way around.

EXERCISES TO INCREASE YOUR SELF-ESTEEM

1. Buy a personal calendar book and put in it only the things you really want to do.
2. Whenever you have a thought that starts with
   'I have to...'
   'I ought to...'
   'I need to...'
   'I should...'
   'I'd better...'
change it to
   'I want to...'
and then ask yourself whether the thought you just had is true.
3. Give yourself the simple pleasures of life in abundance.
   Take a bath daily.
   Stay in bed all day once per week.
   Get a massage weekly.
4. Go first class. Make your meal selections in restaurants by looking only at the left side of the menu. Going first class may take a little practice if lack of money has always been the basis of your financial decisions.

48

5. Always speak the best of yourself and others and expect others to do the same.

6. Find something you like about everyone that you know and everyone that you meet.

7. Schedule time by yourself to think and to write affirmations. This will make it easy to become your own best friend and give up being your own date of last resort.

NOTICE HOW WEALTHY YOU ALREADY ARE

If money is a survival issue for you, it is a good idea to notice that lack of money has not killed you. If you pay taxes in your city, then you own the public transportation systems there. The bus driver is being paid with your money to provide a useful service for you. For fifty cents or so you can ride the bus anytime you want to without worrying about taking care of the bus when you are done using it.

When you spend seventy-five cents for a container of milk at the super market, consider that the super market has thousands of dollars worth of refrigerators there so that you get the milk at exactly the right temperature. The plant where the milk was processed probably has millions of dollars worth of equipment as does the dairy farm of origin. You are able to receive the benefits of all this for 75 cents.

LOTTERIES

Government lotteries are becoming increasingly popular in the U.S. More and more State Governments are turning to lotteries to shore up deficit ridden budgets and to provide much needed money for education. While the motives are laudable, the methods deserve anything but praise. Lottery winners receive disproportionate publicity compared to people who become millionaires by using more conventional and service oriented methods, like starting your own business, for example.

If winning the lottery is the most clearly thought out plan that you have for becoming a millionaire, then you are relying on nothing but blind hope. Effective use of the principles in this book provide you with a far better chance of becoming a millionaire than the State lottery. Many more people become millionaires every year by starting their own business than by winning a lottery, although the self-made millionaires receive far less public attention. Most state governments that conduct lotteries would prosecute you vigorously if you ran a public gambling operation in your home and, at the same time, would tell you that they were serving the public interest by doing so.

Lotteries are a tax on greed, most often paid by the members of society who can least afford it. Don't waste money you could use on something else on the lottery.

LEARNING TO BE OVERPAID

The balance in your bank account right now, the amount of your income last year and everything else about your money can be thought of as the result of an unconscious mental formula—the formula that you have constructed which describes the relationship between the value of your work and what you receive from it. Whether this formula is hereditary or whether it is the result of conditioning by your environment has been the subject of study and debate by behavioral scientists for a long time. The most likely answer is that environment and conditioning both contribute to your behavior.

More important than knowing the origin of the formula is knowing how to change it. It may be somewhat unusual for you to consider that your unconscious mind could have something to do with your financial situation—in other words, it may seem strange to you that thoughts that you do not know about can have an effect on your financial situation. To a certain extent, this entire book is about changing the effect of thoughts that you don't know about upon your financial life. If you consider that your unconscious mind has the ability to digest your dinner, thereby demonstrating its ability to convert a wide range of raw material into fingernails, eyeballs and other parts of your body, it may be easier to understand that thoughts that you do not know about may have something to do with your finances. However the only real proof that you will get will be from experimenting with the methods described herein and being willing for them to work. Affirmations to aid you in changing your unconscious formula:

1) The value of my work is increasing rapidly in everyone's opinion.
2) It is OK for me to be overpaid.
3) I am grateful that my creativity provides me with an endless stream of practical ideas about increasing my income.
4) All shortages are temporary.
5) There are plenty of opportunities for me to serve people and increase my income.

DEMOLISHING A POVERTY CONSCIOUSNESS

Here is an exercise that will rapidly destroy a poverty consciousness. Make a list of your ten most negative ideas about money. Select the most negative one and invert it into an affirmation that you want to work with. Do not be fooled by the simplicity of this exercise. With my consulting clients I have found that this exercise is the most effective one, which is why I have saved it for last.

Here is a space to do this:

Negative thoughts	Affirmations
1.	1.
2.	2.
3.	3.
4.	4.
5.	5.
6.	6.
7.	7.
8.	8.
9.	9.
10.	10.

CHAPTER VI

COMMON CAUSES OF
POVERTY CONSCIOUSNESS

In my consulting work, I have discovered several common causes of poverty consciousness. What follows is a description of each case as well as the affirmations that have enabled people to get free of it. Since everyone is different, this chapter should not be considered to contain all the causes of poverty consciousness. Study the symptoms and see whether they apply to you. If they do, I suggest you use the applicable affirmations.

FAILING TO GET EVEN

This is the most common cause of poverty consciousness. All parents secretly or openly desire their children to be more successful than they are. As children, frequently the only way to get the attention of our parents is to do what they disapprove of. This is certain to bring attention in the form of correction. We resent this correction because no one likes to feel helpless or be told what to do. For most children, it is not safe enough to express this resentment. You may have tried to tell your parents what you thought about their ideas about bringing you up and found the results unpleasant for you. When you grow up it finally becomes safe enough to express the resentment you felt during childhood. An easy way to do this is to fail financially and have your parents live in continuing fear of having to support you or to feel responsible for your failure as you attempt to demonstrate to them what a poor job they did as parents. Failing to get even (I hope you did not miss the play on words) can take forever. Since there is no satisfaction in it, it will never feel like you got even enough. If you resent authority figures, if you resent rich people or if you are one of those people who loves your parents and considers them perfect, then you probably have some of Failing to Get Even.

Affirmations

1. I forgive my parents for their ignorant behavior toward me.
2. It is OK for me to accept love and money now and still get even later if I want to.
3. I now see the humor in using failure to get attention.

FEAR OF LOSS OF PARENTS' LOVE

If there was not much physical affection expressed in your household as a child and instead your parents expressed their love for you by giving you things like cars, vacations and clothes, then you probably have some of this syndrome. Receiving gifts from your parents is the way you get their love, so you keep yourself poor, or at least poorer than they are so you will always be in a position to accept gifts from them. This syndrome sometimes manifests in what I call the Income Ceiling Law. I have worked with clients who several times during their careers have increased their income up to what the maximum family income of their parents was only to have their income inexplicably decrease. To observe this pattern, it is usually necessary to add a couple of thousand dollars per year to the maximum income of the parents to allow for inflation, because it is really income as reflected in standard of living that matters here.

In other cases of this syndrome, people are chronic overachievers, but never seem to be satisfied. This is you if you are your own worst critic.

Affirmations

1. I am lovable whether or not I am successful.
2. I am grateful for the challenge of taking care of myself.
3. It is OK and safe for me to make more money than my parents.

INHERITED MONEY

It is not necessary to come from a family where large inheritances are part of the family tradition or to ever have received an inheritance in order to have this syndrome. If as a small child, you were promised an inheritance of $500 that probably sounded like a huge fortune to you at the time. It is interesting to notice that in families where inheritances are part of the family tradition, frequently everyone knows how much everyone will receive when everyone dies; yet everyone claims they never talk about it. A family tradition of inherited money frequently involves guilt, helplessness and loss associated with money. I have seen people who have been promised small inheritances feel so guilty about just the prospect of profiting from the loss of a loved one that they kept themselves poor for years so they could feel like they would deserve the inheritance when it came.

Additionally the prospect of a large inheritance can cause the prospective recipient to conclude, "Why bother?" about creating an income for himself. In 1905, William Vanderbilt was quoted as saying, "Inherited wealth is a big handicap to happiness. It is as certain death to ambition as cocaine is to morality."

Unraveling this syndrome is a two-step process. The first step is to take responsibility for the money that you have received as an inheritance so that you can resolve the guilt and helplessness surrounding it. The second step is to dissolve the subconscious association between dollars and death. Here are some affirmations so that you can do that:

1. I deserve to be prosperous and wealthy.
2. It is OK for me to receive love and money from various people and places at once.
3. My wealth contributes to my aliveness and to the aliveness of others.

HELPLESSNESS

Helplessness is the thought that you can't get what you want—or that getting what you want is so difficult that it is not worth it. If, as a child, rewards were always contingent upon the performance of some unpleasant task—no allowance until you mow the lawn, no ice cream until you eat your lima beans, then you probably have some of this syndrome. The basic idea is that in order to get what you want, you have to give up your freedom. Obviously your freedom is more valuable than money, so the tendency here is to stay poor.

Affirmations
1. My wealth contributes to my freedom and my freedom contributes to my wealth.
2. I have enough time, energy, wisdom and money to accomplish all my desires.

WOMEN AND MONEY

I have worked with women whose only negative idea about money is that money is something that men do, and women should have nothing to do with it. Women's liberation notwithstanding, if you are a woman, you probably grew up with different ideas about money than your twin brother did or than your twin brother would have if you had had one. Money responds to the commands of your mind and it knows nothing of your gender. There is nothing to stop you from becoming a millionaire and keeping your sexual attractiveness, too. The archetype of the mindless housewife is fast disappearing from the American scene. Even when it existed, the mindless housewife was not so mindless as she was led to believe; it is just that she forgot to acknowledge herself for the managerial skill she exhibited in orchestrating the complex transportation, food service, entertainment and personal counselling business required to run a home.

Affirmations
1. I am no longer a helpless victim. I have the right to tell myself and others what to do.
2. I am not my mother. I am a financially successful business woman.
3. It is fun for me to be a wealthy woman.

MEN AND MONEY

If you are a man, you may feel that you have been blessed with more training about money than your sisters. Unfortunately, if you think about it, you will discover that the majority of this training is negative, and has to do with struggle and control. A common idea held by men is that if they amass a fortune, it will ensure their financial security and they will then be able to relax. Since most tension is psychosomatic, rather than financial, they don't feel anymore relaxed after they have the money.

Affirmations
1. I feel safe whether I am in control or not.
2. Past negative experiences no longer detract from my financial success.
3. It is fun for me to be a wealthy man.

DEBT AS A CONDITION OF LIFE

If your parents were in debt until they died and it was only the life insurance money that solved their financial problems, you may have this syndrome. It is your fear of death that is keeping you in debt.

Affirmations
1. My income exceeds my expenses whether I like it or not.
2. I forgive my parents for their financial problems.
3. I am a financial success since my income has exceeded $_ this year. (Insert the amount of income you have received in the past 12 months in the affirmation.)

UNDERNOURISHMENT SYNDROME

If you were not breast fed as an infant or were fed on a pre-determined schedule, you may have some of this syndrome. You may have concluded "There is not enough milk" or "I have to wait for what I want." These ideas are later translated into "There is not enough money."

People with this syndrome often have an abundance of money everywhere but in their pocket or experience widely varying income patterns from month to month. The basic idea here is that nourishment is something beyond your control.

Affirmations

1. I forgive my mother for her unwillingness to nourish me at birth.
2. I am now certain that there is enough for me.
3. I forgive myself for thinking that my mother used deprivation to control me; I now appreciate her generosity and co-operation.

CHAPTER VII

COUPLES AND MONEY

Money is consistently named as the leading cause of divorce. It is doubtful that too much money would drive a couple apart. Too little money may cause some depression and disappointment, but not necessarily a divorce. The inability to discuss money without fighting and the inability to contribute to each other's financial well being is what causes problems.

The safety that we experience in intimate relationships frequently permits thoughts and feelings to come to the surface that remain suppressed in other relationships. The best financial arrangements for your household can be gained by experimentation. Most people handle money in their relationships the same way that their parents did. Unless your parents' financial life was totally harmonious, then it might be worthwhile to experiment a little. Parental arguments about money often leave people with the idea that money is not a socially acceptable topic of conversation because of the upsets that seem to be caused by discussing it.

If you find it impossible to discuss money with your romantic partner, then important financial decisions and spending behavior will be determined by your momentary emotions and unconscious thinking patterns rather than by the effective alignment of your decisions and behavior with your financial goals. It is essential to manage your finances in a businesslike way if you desire to achieve more and accumulate more.

Successful negotiation can be accomplished by having a financial discussion with your partner at regularly scheduled intervals (the beginning of the month is usually a good time). At this discussion, make agreements about who will pay how much of each of the expenses. This is a reasonably risk free way to do it, even if both of you are afraid of negotiating, because the agreement only lasts for a month. At the beginning of the next month you will have had a month's experience with the agreement you made and an opportunity to make a different one or just change parts of it.

Many couples find it difficult to discuss money issues in a straightforward and honest way. A comment I frequently hear is "Talking about money always leads to a fight." It is essential that you practice the following suggestions so that you and your partner can learn to discuss your finances without criticizing each other and yelling at each other. If you don't, then you won't get much more money than you already have. In other words, as long as you believe that money leads to fights, you may conclude: if we have more money, then we'll have more fights. This conclusion can result in unconscious sabotage of even the best made plans to accumulate wealth.

If the woman is the one who stays at home and takes care of the house and the man is the only income producer, then it is reasonable for her to receive a salary for the household managerial services she provides. If he objects, then she can suggest that he look in the local newspaper to find out how much live-in maids cost these days. Conversely, if the man is the only income producer and pays the rent or mortgage payments; then there is no reason that the woman should not pay rent out of her salary. I always recommend that both people in an intimate relationship have their own checking and savings accounts. Joint checking usually turns into a race—a race to see who can spend the money first or a race to see who can be the more martyr-like about not spending it.

It is inevitable that you and your partner will have disagreements from time to time about money and about other issues as well. If two people agree on everything, you can be sure that one of them is doing all the thinking. The purpose of the methods described in this chapter is to enable you to reduce conflict about finances, resolve quickly the conflicts that do occur and to enable you to contribute to each other in defining and accomplishing your goals. If the financial values of your spouse are vastly different from yours then you are bound to have problems unless you can reconcile the differences. To state an extreme example, if one partner insists on saving every spare penny to buy a house and the other insists on spending every spare penny gambling at the local race track, then resolution of these differing values is an essential pre-requisite to financial harmony and co-operation. That two people with such greatly different financial values would marry each other or stay married for very long is unlikely.

Most couples already have substantial agreement about financial values and some differences. Learning to contribute to each other's financial success involves identification of similar values and minimization of the conflict caused by differing values. Keeping all of your money in joint accounts makes each and every expenditure a source of potential conflict. If each partner has agreed upon money of his own that he or she can spend, save or invest without justification or explanation, then the potential for conflict is greatly reduced. Keeping all of your money in joint accounts is most often a sign that a couple is not effectively discussing their finances and is also a source of conflict. Many couples who keep all of their money in joint accounts do so simply because their parents did and have not considered alternatives. If your parents had a less harmonious relationship regarding money issues than you would like to have, surely it is time for you to consider alternatives.

MANAGING YOUR MONEY IN A BUSINESSLIKE WAY

A successful business endeavors to increase its profits by finding new and better ways to serve new and existing customers with the products and services that it offers by finding ways to deliver its products in a low cost, high quality way and by developing new and improved products and services to contribute to increased income in the future. Regarding your personal finances, effective co-ordination of these activities and making the best trade offs to define and accomplish your goals

61

requires frequent discussion with your partner, just as business people require frequent meetings to co-ordinate their activities. The essential difference in a romantic relationship is that there is no legitimate authority. A romantic relationship is a partnership of equals and therefore functions best by agreement. Businesses are invariably structured as hierarchies where some people have authority over others. Financial harmony and co-ordination in a romantic relationship therefore requires even more communication than in a business.

SCHEDULE AND HOLD MONTHLY FINANCIAL COMMITTEE MEETINGS WITH YOUR MATE

You'll probably require two hours or so for each meeting. Discuss financial matters only at your committee meetings. Prepare and agree upon agenda topics beforehand. If topics unrelated to your financial situation come up during the meeting, postpone them for future discussion. At the first meeting, start with full disclosure about your financial situation, if you have not already done so with your mate. If you already enjoy complete financial disclosure then this first step can be used as an update.

If you do not have a complete and up to date statement of assets, liabilities, income and expenses, then agreeing on who will prepare this and when must be a topic at your first meeting. If your finances are complicated, you may wish to hire an accountant or bookkeeper to help you with this.

There must be clear agreement on job assignments—who deals with the stock broker, the creditors and the bank accounts. Full disclosure is an important element. Discovering that your mate has $50,000 stashed in an undisclosed bank account is likely to be just as upsetting as finding out that there is a $50,000 undisclosed debt.

Secrecy about money is an aspect of conditioning learned from parents who didn't know how to discuss money openly. Even most major companies display great anxiety about disclosing the salaries of their employees. You will undoubtedly stir up some trouble if you propose to your boss or the president of your company that the salaries of all employees be posted on the bulletin board. The anxious reaction of business managers to this idea is usually quite extreme when you consider that the salaries of the top officers in any publicly held company are routinely subject to public disclosure in financial reports required by the United States Securities and Exchange Commission and that the pay rates of union workers are often announced in news releases.

For a while, I experimented with asking people, "What is your income?" If the person didn't know me very well, a frequent response was "It's none of your business!" in an indignant tone of voice. Perhaps they are right, perhaps their income is in fact none of my business; however, if you think about it, most of the things that people disclose about themselves in social conversation (their desires, their goals, their experiences, etc.) are really none of your business either. Clearly it is neither necessary nor advisable to discuss your money situation with everyone you meet; the point is that if talking about money or thinking about money makes you uncomfortable, then you are reducing your chances of getting more of it.

Once you have a written statement of your current financial situation, you can begin defining your financial goals, making decisions to accomplish them and begin discussing other creative ways that you can apply together the principles in this book.

Effective money management is not a luxury only for the wealthy. If you wait until you are rich to begin to manage your money wisely, it is unlikely that you'll get rich. Even if you do, the cost of your sloppy money management habits will increase with your wealth.

ACKNOWLEDGE YOUR FEARS ABOUT GETTING RICH

You may be a whole lot more aware of your fears about going broke than of your fears of getting rich. Almost everyone fears change, because it is unknown—even changes for the better. Often women are afraid that their husband will leave them once he gets rich and men are afraid that they will lose control of their wife once she experiences the independence of succeeding on her own. Take a moment to consider your fears about having an immediate and permanent hundredfold increase in your income and discuss these with your partner. Verbal sentence completion processes aid greatly in uncovering and acknowledging suppressed emotions. Spend two minutes repeating to your partner, "A fear I have about getting rich is _____" and ask your partner to respond to each repetition simply with "Thank you" and no additional comment. Complete the sentence by filling in the blank with whatever comes to your mind without rehearsal. Ask your partner to do the same with you.

FIND WORK THAT YOU LOVE

It is impossible to enjoy your life very much with the "Thank God It's Friday" Attitude. Unless your work is a source of satisfaction, an outlet for your creativity and an expression of your important values, you are making unreasonable demands on the rest of your life to satisfy you. If you are like most people, you spend more time working than any other activity except sleeping. At worst, your job is an expression of how much you need money. Having work that you do not like places undue stress on your family relationships. If you do not have work that you love, begin immediately by doing The Perfect Career Exercise in Chapter V.

PRENUPTIAL AGREEMENTS

A prenuptial agreement is a legal contract that defines the division of individual assets in the event of divorce. Without a prenuptial agreement, the division of assets in the event of divorce is likely to be determined by the laws of your State as interpreted by a divorce court; in other words, you may have little to say about the outcome. The idea of a prenuptial agreement may threaten dearly held romantic illusions; however, the practicality of such an agreement, especially for people who have or plan on having substantial income and assets, far exceeds the value of romantic notions.

The process of negotiating a prenuptial agreement may well be more important than the agreement itself. If you find that it is impossible to negotiate a prenuptial agreement with your prospective marriage partner, then it is unlikely that the two of you will have much success in resolving financial disagreements once you are married. The icy effect of negotiating can be reduced by including in the agreement statements about your financial goals and how money will be managed during your marriage.

TEACHING YOUR CHILDREN ABOUT MONEY

In human and in animal societies, full grown individuals accept the task of caring for their young. The instincts that motivate creatures to the accomplishment of this task are built into the genes of any reasonably complicated species that survives longer than one generation. The ability to provide for oneself distinguishes between adults from children. Children lack money, power and skills. The task of a parent is to assist and guide the development of a helpless, inept and financially poor infant into a healthy, happy, productive, independent and prosperous adult. For reasons that are as mysterious to me as the desire to have children, many parents seem to invest the majority of their energy regarding their children into encouraging them to conform to prescribed standards of behavior rather than encouraging their creativity and self-esteem.

The majority of important lessons that children learn are learned from the example that their parents provide about how to be an adult. Actions speak louder than words. Parental love and caring is far more valuable to children than anything that money can buy for them. It is not your job as a parent to deprive yourself of the things that you want so that your children can have what they want. If you do this, you will provide your children with the example that the way to be an adult is to sacrifice for your children. Your children, in this instance, will not want to grow up and will probably be asking you for money long after they have reached maturity.

Teach your children how to manage their own money. Let them experiment with a wide variety of jobs and businesses before they become concerned with building a stable resume, give them the opportunity to learn from their mistakes about spending and saving. Children have a natural knack for selling, before it is repressed, usually by the stifling conformity of teenage peer pressure. Encourage your children in their financial ventures and in the enjoyment of the rewards that they receive.

CHAPTER VIII

The Spending Law

The SPENDING LAW can also be called the Exchanging Law or the Giving Law. The SPENDING LAW STATED IS—

THE VALUE OF MONEY IS DETERMINED BY THE BUYER AND SELLER IN EVERY TRANSACTION.

Mastery of this law will relieve you from guilt about money from the fear of cheating others and from the fear of being cheated yourself.

Affirmations regarding the SPENDING LAW
1. My income now exceeds my expenses.
2. The more willing I am to prosper others, the more willing others are to prosper me.
3. Every dollar I spend comes back to me multiplied.

Affirmations regarding the SPENDING LAW—explained

"My income now exceeds my expenses." A basic principle about money is that you must receive it before you spend it. This means that you have and have always had a positive cash flow. If you have money in your pocket, in your piggy bank, in your checking account or anywhere else, then that money is the degree to which your cash flow is positive. Even after you pay your bills, your cash flow is positive. Banks make it easy for you to see this, because if you pay bills in excess of the cash in your checking account, they will return some checks to you with a note that says in effect "Since you always have a positive cash flow, it is impossible for us to pay these checks yet." Bills and debts are not expenses, they are agreements. Bills and debts do not become expenses until you pay them. You will find practical ideas for handling bills and debts in the next chapter which is about budgeting. My income now exceeds my expenses happens to be the truth about money whether you like it or not. Working with this affirmation will incorporate it into your consciousness at the emotional level.

"The more willing I am to prosper others, the more willing others are to prosper me." The essence of practicing this idea is the act of generosity. Generosity is the willingness to give money cheerfully to people that do not need it. Almost everyone gives money to people that do not need it, with varying degrees of cheerfulness. Probably most of the bills you pay and many of the checks you write and much of the cash you spend go to people who do not need your money. You can expect the Telephone Company or the holders of your student loan to take all possible steps to collect the money that you owe them; however very few of the people and companies where you spend your money would be seriously damaged if you were never to pay up. So, you are practicing generosity more than you think. It will cost you no more to be cheerful about it. Generosity is different from the practice of charity which is the willingness to give money cheerfully to people that do need it. Charity is a wonderful idea and a noble practice, but it will not get you out of need of money. Generosity is the fastest way I can think of to get out of need for money. Need equals lack equals shortage. Sometimes people think their need for money is what creates money for them. This idea makes it difficult to give up your need because you are certain if you give up your need for money, it will stop coming to you. It's unlikely that you'll ever have much money if it's not OK for you to have more than you need. Cheerfully giving money to people who don't need it will dissolve any mental association you may have between money and need.

"Every dollar I spend comes back to me multiplied." The concept behind this affirmation is profit. Spending money puts it into circulation and the dollar that you spend goes through many transactions before it returns to you. Each transaction produces a profit. Profit is the multiplication factor that operates on your expenses so that more will return to you. Profit can be defined as the creation of new wealth by the arbitrary decree of the individual business person. If you buy something for fifty cents and sell it for a dollar, your profit is 50%, but you could have sold it for 60 cents or for $10, in which case your profit would have been different. People with a job, who sell their services, receive a financial profit of 100%.

PRICES

The topic of prices deserves explanation because it is a source of confusion about money. If you visit the local hamburger stand and ask why a Super Burger with Cheese costs 89 cents, you might get an answer like—'Well, we take the cost of the meat, the cost of the bun, the cost of the tomato and add them up and multiply the sum by 1.2. Then we take the cost of the rent, the cost of the people to cook and serve it, and the cost of the electricity; we add these numbers together and multiply the sum by 1.3. The final step is to take the two final numbers and add them together which produces an answer which produces 89 cents. So that is why Super Burgers with Cheese cost 89 cents.'

If you examine this answer a little, you will discover the truth about prices. This is that all prices are arbitrary. Even the prices that are determined by formula (as just described) are arbitrary because the formulas are arbitrary. Considering the case of the Super Burger with Cheese, the costs that are included and omitted from the formula are arbitrary, the factors in the formula are arbitrary, and the allocation of common costs to each product is arbitrary. In fact, if you visit another hamburger stand across the street from the first one, you may get an entirely different answer whether their price for a Super Burger with Cheese is the same or different.

NEGOTIATION

Since all prices are arbitrary, then all prices are negotiable. In fact, everything in the physical universe is negotiable. Negotiation is the process whereby both parties to a transaction get what they want. In economic terms negotiation is the practice that converts the general marketplace to the specific marketplace. More than one person is required for there to be a transaction. Transactions never occur without the agreement of two or more people. Anyone who has ever been involved in a real estate transaction is aware of this. You can make a detailed study of the real estate market in your neighborhood to arrive at the best asking price for your house. All of that study does not do you a bit of good until you have an offer from a buyer; from someone who agrees with you. The secret of negotiation is to find out what you want and ask for it, then find out what the other person wants and figure out a way to give that in exchange. I find it unusual that it is more socially acceptable to complain about what you have than it is to ask for what you want.

The fear of being trapped into a deal that they don't like is what prevents most people from negotiating. You have the right to say no at any point in a negotiation, whether you explain the reason for the no or not. Additionally, all agreements are subject to renegotiation at any point. You could not make an agreement unless you had the power to make agreements and making an agreement does not take away that power.

CREDIT

There are several paradoxes about credit. Credit is for people who don't need it, it is for people with enough imagination to put the money that they borrow to effective use. If you don't believe this, try to get a loan without filling out an application that describes how you will repay the money. This is an unintentional attempt on the part of the banks to teach you the principles in this book.

Conversely, if you borrow enough money from the bank and you have trouble making the payments, the bank will loan you more so you can make the payments. This is because you have gotten to the point where they can't afford to have you go under.

The best policy regarding credit is to pay cash for everything except self-liquidating assets. This means you have to figure out how to create a profit on any item that you borrowed money for so you can repay the loan and have some extra for yourself. Personal charge cards are the bane of people with a poverty consciousness. If charge cards are a problem for you, I recommend that you cut them up in little pieces and immediately begin the practice of paying cash for everything except self-liquidating assets. Master Charge is a wonderful idea, but if you are buying things that you would not otherwise buy because you have the card, then the card is the master of you instead of the other way around. *In Think and Grow Rich* Napoleon Hill wrote "The spendthrift cannot succeed, mainly because he stands eternally in fear of poverty. Form the habit of systematic saving by putting aside a definite percentage of your income. Money in the bank gives one a very safe foundation.... Without money, one must take what one is offered, and be glad of it."

$100 BILL

This little idea is great for people who are always saying 'I don't have any money.' Visit the bank and get a $100 bill and carry it in your pocket or purse. You can spend it whenever you want to so long as you can replace it from the bank immediately. If you follow this practice, you will never be broke again. You will never get down to your last dollar. The closest you will ever get to being broke is your last $100. The reason that people stay broke for so long is that it is depressing to be broke, however it is difficult to be depressed about money with $100 in your pocket. If $100 is too scary for you, you can start the practice with a silver dollar or a two dollar bill and graduate yourself upwards as you become more confident with money.

TAXES, ECONOMICS, AND THE MONEY SYSTEM

It is a popular practice of financially unsuccessful people to blame the government for their financial problems. A study of economic history will indicate that there have been a wide variety of political philosophies and economic doctrines that have achieved popularity in different countries at different times. Despite all this, there have always been some people with more money than others. It is impossible to make any economic system the cause of financial success or failure.

Money was invented by people for their own convenience. $100 dollar bills are easier to carry around, to exchange and to store than the goods and services that they represent. Articles of value in any economy are the goods and services that the people exchange with each other. Money is the *measure* not the essence of this value.

If the economic system were to disappear then someone would have to re-invent another one. I like to ask people who blame the economic system for their problems what it is that makes them think they will do any better with a different system.

Inflation is an obvious example of the power of the human mind over money. Inflation occurs because everyone thinks that it will. This expectation makes it a self-fulfilling prophecy.

It is interesting to me that those who complain the most about taxes claim not to be interested in politics. If having 30-50% of your income taken out of your pay check before you even see it is not enough to get you interested in politics, what will it take? The validity of your complaints about the government is questionable if you do not vote. The wisdom of your opinions is wasted if you do not communicate them to your elected representatives.

TITHING

Tithing is an ancient prosperity principle. Tithing is regularly giving away ten percent of your income. Giving away ten percent of your income produces several beneficial effects. This practice provides the opportunity to confront any thoughts you may have about lack of money, it helps you feel that you actually own the remaining ninety percent of your income instead of having your income already "spoken for" by other people, and it helps to free you from needing money.

CHAPTER IX

The Monthly Percentage Budget

Why make and use a budget? When I announce the segment on budgeting in the seminars that I conduct, there is often an initial negative reaction among the participants (audible groans). They tell me that this is because they associate a budget with deprivation. In other words they think a budget will deprive them of what they want and cause them to manage their money the way they should. This kind of thinking is foolish, because you are the one that makes your budget and you can arrange it in the way that pleases you the most. Without a budget, your spending patterns will tend to conform to unconsciously chosen patterns of conformity or rebellion left over from childhood. Since we are not aware of these patterns (although an analysis of how you spend your money will make them evident), the purchases that we make as a result of following unconscious patterns do not satisfy our conscious desires. Another way to say this is that everyone is already spending his money according to a budget; the question is whether the budget is unconsciously chosen by past conditioning or consciously chosen based on current goals and values. A budget provides you with an opportunity to declare your CONSCIOUSLY chosen spending patterns and to spend your money to satisfy your conscious desires and values.

Creating a budget forces you to examine how you really spend your money. Frequently people possess unacknowledged shame about their spending which is activated by the budgeting process. Your current net worth and the balance in your savings account are the result of whatever budget you have been using in the past. Whether you are satisfied with the results of your

73

budget is solely up to you. You can get an idea of this by comparing the amount of money you have earned throughout your life to your net worth or savings balance and see how you feel about the effectiveness of your budgeting so far.

A common excuse that some people use to avoid having a consciously prepared budget is, "I have to spend everything I make just to get by, so a budget would be of no use to me." My suggestion is do not wait until you have a lot of money before you learn to manage it well. Once you do get a lot of money, you won't have it for very long if you don't know how to manage it.

The purpose of the Monthly Percentage Budget is to realize that you are in charge of your money. Dollar Budgets do not work because they operate from scarcity. If you ever did a dollar budget, you probably thought 'Since I do not have enough money, I'd better make a budget.' After adding up your expenses, you found out that your worst fears were true, that you really didn't have enough money. A percentage budget will work for you every time if you practice it faithfully. This is because it starts with the idea of abundance; your income will never go below 100%. Another important result that the budget will produce for you is certainty about your ability to live abundantly within your means no matter what your means may be. This is important because without this certainty, money is always an emergency for you and it is more difficult to produce creative ideas in an emergency.

The first step in the creation of a Monthly Percentage Budget is to make a list of the items that you spend money for. Consolidate these categories into logical classifications so that there are approximately 8-10 categories.

Sample Monthly Percentage Budget

Savings	10%
Debts	20%
Gifts	10%
Taxes	15%
Housing	15%
Self-Improvement	10%
Food	12%

Transportation & Communication	<u>8%</u>
Total	100%

The second step is to assign percentages of your monthly income to spend in each of these categories as shown in the sample. I was so unconscious about my expenses that I found it necessary to keep a record of all the cash that I spent for a month before I felt confident enough to prepare a Monthly Percentage Budget.

The final step is the ongoing practice of finding ways that you can reduce your expenditure in each category while at the same time living better in that category. A good way is to select one category and think about it until you have successfully produced a surplus in that category before moving on to the next one. Once you have figured out how to live better in one category for less money, you have secured a surplus for yourself in that category for future months because you will certainly not want to go back to whatever you were doing before which not only cost more but produced less satisfaction.

Remember, every time you spend money, you increase the income of someone else. Taken to an extreme, if you had a successful business in every area where you now spend money, it would be possible to reduce your expenses to zero.

EXPLANATION OF ITEMS IN THE SAMPLE MONTHLY PERCENTAGE BUDGET

SAVINGS

Once you develop the habit of saving 10% of your income you will never be without money. As shown in the budget it is important to save the first 10% of your income. This is merely building the habit of paying yourself first. Do not wait until you can afford to save 10% before beginning this practice. Actually you cannot afford not to begin this practice immediately, if you haven't already done so. This is because saving regularly is an affirmation that you have a surplus of cash which will have a favorable effect on your income. Do not wait until you are out of debt to become a successful saver.

DEBTS

If you have debts, then I suggest that you put aside no more than 20% of your monthly income for debt payments. It is a good idea to make regular payments to each one of your creditors, no matter how small the payments are. If you have a debt that you are not making payments on, it is very easy to see how long it will take you to repay it at that rate. The answer is **FOREVER.** If the monthly payments on your debts exceed 20% of your income, then it becomes necessary to negotiate with your creditors and to work out a payment plan that will enable you to win. Sometimes I have seen people continue to make large regular payments on their debts which they could ill afford solely in order to protect their credit rating. If you have debt problems, the last thing you need to worry about is your credit rating which got you into the mess in the first place. In fact, honest communication with your creditors and regular monthly payments, both of which are indications of your ability and willingness to repay, may improve your credit rating.

GIFTS

Having gifts as a category in your budget will enable you to practice tithing as described in the previous chapter.

TAXES

If you are self-employed, then it is a good idea to put aside a portion of your income for taxes, so that you have money to pay them when the time comes. It is much easier to negotiate with the IRS for a lower tax bill if you are not starting at the point of being unable to pay what the IRS may think you owe. If your employer withholds income taxes from your salary then this category is taken care of for you.

HOUSING

There are a myriad of ways to reduce your housing expense and to live better. Here is a list of some of the ideas that people have used. You can pick one or more that you like or invent your own according to personal preference. Acquire enough real estate so that the income from it pays your rent, find a housemate that you like, use your house for your business or buy your own home if you now rent, make energy saving investments in your home.

SELF-IMPROVEMENT

Self-improvement is the best investment you can make because you are investing directly in yourself. Conversely, rent is the worst investment you can make, because all you get is shelter for 30 days. At the end of the month your landlord wants some more money. The money you spent on this book, on other self-improvement books and on self-improvement seminars and courses will provide you dividends forever and at no extra charge. Any good self-improvement course will result in an increase in income, along with additional personal benefits.

CLOTHING

Here again are some ideas that people have used to have better clothing and to spend less. Make your own, find a job you like better that requires cheaper clothing, select a clothing store and tell them how much you want to spend on clothing every month and say you are willing to spend it all at their store if they will give you a discount. When you find a store that will agree to it, open a charge account and mail them the money in your clothing budget every month. When you want to go shopping, simply look at the credit balance in your charge account to see how much you have to spend.

FOOD

Most Americans over eat, yet are under nourished. Experiment with more fresh fruits and vegetables and grains in your diet and I would be surprised if you didn't feel better and spend less.

I know of a woman in New York who visited Tiffany's and ordered engraved invitations that invited her to dinner. She mailed them out to all her friends and asked them to fill in a date and time that was convenient for them and to mail them back to her. This is surely an act of high self-esteem. Those who think that their company is a nuisance would never think of something like this.

TRANSPORTATION AND COMMUNICATION

Car pool, hitchhike, buy your plane tickets far enough in advance to get a discount, fly at night, carry interesting things to sell on the plane, make your phone calls at night, call collect, use the mail system instead of the phone, etc., etc.

The fact that most of us are pretty unconscious about what we spend our money on makes it easy for a percentage budget to have a dramatic and rapid effect on your expenses. There is no limit to the ideas that will work for you here. If you think that some of your expenses are fixed, then ask yourself who it was that fixed them.

LIVING WITHIN YOUR MEANS

The primary benefit of learning to manage your money with a percentage budget is that it provides you with a concrete experience of living within your means. Another way to say this is that it enables you to keep your boat afloat until your ship comes in. Often study, time and practice are required for people to incorporate the principles in this book into their lives. Increasing your income requires a proper combination of the right thoughts and effective direct action. This means that it is likely that you will have to get along on your current income for a while until the principles in this book begin to pay off for you.

An important paradox about money is that in one sense the supply is unlimited. If the money flow was halted long enough to count it all, clearly the resulting answer would be a large finite number. However, circulation makes the finite amount of money infinite for all practical purpose. In another sense, the money that anyone has at any given moment is limited and for this reason, it is essential to develop the discipline of not spending or committing to spend money that you do not have.

As a nation, twentieth century Americans are chronically the least thrifty savers among industrial countries. The Federal budget deficit appears to be a collective reflection of American habits and attitudes of get it now and pay for it someday.

Living within your means offers many important advantages over having to spend substantial portions of your current income to finance past purchases. Some of these are:

1) Peace of mind.

2) Ability to turn down good income opportunities in order to develop or await better ones.

3) The freedom to spend your income however you wish.

It is unwise to rely upon the credit system to prevent you from becoming over-extended. Financial institutions exhibit an unusual willingness to loan out money in greater quantities that people can repay. In the early 1980's, I spent a couple of years travelling and conducting seminars without a fixed address. In 1982, I settled down in Los Angeles. After a few months there, I realized that I had allowed all of my magazine subscriptions to expire soon after I had begun travelling. I subscribed to several magazines that interested me. One of the magazines made a typographical error in my name and addressed its magazines to Phil LaNut. They got my address right so the magazines arrived regularly. Soon, I began to receive junk mail addressed to Phil LaNut and I realized that magazines commonly sell their subscriber lists to other companies for use in direct mail advertising. One day I received a letter addressed to Phil LaNut from one of the largest banks in the country. The letter began: "Dear Phil LaNut, Because of your outstanding credit record, you have been pre-approved for a _____ Bank VISA card. Simply sign and return the enclosed application and your new VISA card with its many benefits can soon be yours."

GETTING OUT OF DEBT

If the monthly payments on your installment credit loans (excluding the payment on your home mortgage, which counts as housing expense) exceed 20% of your income, you have a debt problem whether you realize it or not. As mentioned earlier in this chapter, it is imprudent to rely on your creditors to prevent you from accumulating more debt than you can afford to repay. The downward spiral begins with more debt than you can handle, resulting in higher monthly payments than you can afford, resulting in additional borrowing to pay expenses because of the cash shortage caused by the high monthly payments. Decisive and often drastic action is essential to change this. The problem will not solve itself despite your most earnest hopes. The sooner that you take decisive action, the easier it will be. Every moment that you delay makes the solution more difficult.

STEP 1. Stop borrowing. Pay cash for everything. Slice up your credit cards into little pieces.

STEP 2. Modify your budget and spending behavior. Even the most drastic steps are worthwhile to reduce your current expenses to 70% of your income, leaving 20% for debt repayment and 10% for savings. If you don't know where the money goes, get a small notebook and write down every penny you spend for a month. This record plus your checkbook register will give you a clear picture of your expenses.

STEP 3. Begin saving immediately. Working merely to get out of debt is not very inspiring. Do not wait until you are out of debt to begin saving. Start now. You can't afford not to. The surplus that you generate by saving will have a beneficial effect on your attitude about money, aiding you in increasing your income.

STEP 4. Spend no more than 20% of your income on reducing your debts. If your required monthly payments (excluding home mortgage payment) exceed 20% of your income, then pay each of your creditors as much as you can up to, but not beyond 20% of your income. Communicate with your creditors to explain why you are doing this, and assuring them that you will pay them as soon as you can. Clearly there is a risk that your credit rating will suffer temporarily. This is a minor disadvantage compared to the benefits of getting out of debt. Staying broke merely to preserve the credit rating that enabled you to create the problem in the first place is manifestly foolish. Additionally, with money in the bank, your credit rating will be of less concern to you.

In addition to the information in this book, help is available without charge from Debtors Anonymous, a world wide network of approximately 160 support groups based on the Alcoholics Anonymous Twelve Step Program. To locate a Debtors Anonymous group in your area consult the white pages of your local telephone directory or call directory assistance. If you get no results there, write to:

Debtors Anonymous
PO Box 20322
New York, NY 10025-9992

and request a starter kit.

CHAPTER X

The Saving Law

Before describing how to make the Saving Law work for you, I want to state very clearly what I mean by saving. Saving is NOT getting $2000 cash back on the purchase of a new car and using the $2000 for the down payment. Saving is not buying something on sale. Advertisers attempt to convince us that we are saving money when we purchase an item on sale; however that is not what I mean by saving. Americans are historically poor savers. The U.S. is always at the bottom of the list among industrialized countries in statistics about the percentage of personal income that is saved. National budget deficits seem to reflect our personal habits.

By saving I mean setting aside money for a specific use in the future. No matter how you earn your money, it comes to you in certain amounts, rather than in a continuous stream. Almost everyone wants to purchase some item that costs more than the size of the average amount of money that he receives at one time. In order to do this, you have two options. One is to borrow the money to make the purchase and repay the loan by repaying the lender a portion of your future chunks of income, plus interest. The other is to set aside part of each of a series of chunks of income until you have accumulated enough money to buy what you desire. The only APPARENT differences of these two methods are that the borrowing method enables you to make the purchase sooner, in exchange for the extra expense of the interest paid to the lender. There is another substantial difference that may be less than obvious if you are in the habit of making major purchases on time payments. This is peace of mind. When you pay cash for purchases, you do not have to worry about making payments, and you have the freedom of being able to spend all of your income however you want.

THE SAVING LAW can also be called the Storing Law or the Surplus Law. **THE SAVING LAW** is storing away part of your current income for the purpose of future leisure or to increase your future income. If you have the ability to save regularly it is an indication that you are at least as intelligent as a squirrel who stores away nuts for the winter. The Federal Savings and Loan League tells me that most people are not apparently this intelligent. In a recent survey of thousands of savings accounts, the Federal Savings and Loan League discovered that 90% of the accounts surveyed were dormant after being open for six months. This means they had a balance of $10 or less and that there was no one making deposits or withdrawals. So, if you master saving you will become a member of the elite.

If you want to, you can depress yourself into becoming a successful saver by adding up all the money you have ever earned and comparing that to the balance in your savings account.

I think that the reason that so many people fail at savings is because they have only one savings account. If you only have one savings account then it is likely that you are saving without purpose or you are saving for the money. I would call this hoarding or saving for a rainy day or saving motivated by fear of running out. Additionally, if you have only one savings account, then it is likely that you have not given yourself permission to spend the money in it for a specific purpose. So, if you are going to shame yourself for spending the money that you have saved, why bother in the first place? The secret of saving successfully and easily is to have multiple savings accounts each with a special purpose and to give yourself permission to spend the money on what you are saving for, once you have accumulated enough. Here is a list of the seven savings accounts that I recommend. A little later I will describe the secrets of each one.

1. Cash Flow Savings Account
2. Large Purchases Savings Account
3. Financial Independence Savings Account
4. Millionaire's Savings Account
5. Annual Income Savings Account
6. Taxes Savings Account
7. Generosity Savings Account

CASH FLOW SAVINGS ACCOUNT

The Cash Flow Savings Account is basic training in saving. If you deposit your income into your checking account then you must make another decision to save any of it. This is because as everyone knows, checking accounts are for spending, not for saving. If you have followed the practice of depositing your income to your checking account, paying your bills and then intending to save what is left over, you probably already know that there is rarely much left over to save. A Cash Flow Savings Account will put an end to hand to mouth finances. You use this account by depositing all of your income into your Cash Flow Savings Account as soon as you receive it. When you want money for your budget or to feed your other savings accounts, then make a withdrawal and distribute the money to your checking account and other savings accounts. The key is to *always make the withdrawals smaller than the deposits*. When you follow this practice, inexorable mathematical law will cause the balance in this account to increase. Soon the increasing balance in your Cash Flow Savings Account will be a month's income. Having a balance equivalent to a month's income in your Cash Flow Savings Account will make a significant contribution toward your being able to stop worrying about money. I suggest that on the first of the month, you withdraw your month's income from your Cash Flow Savings Account and deposit it into your checking account. At this point, you can be certain of having no financial problems at all for thirty days. During the month you can use the money in your checking account for your budget and can be depositing your income into your cash flow account which will be intact at the beginning of the next month. To some this may sound like financial hocus pocus, which it is until you examine the psychological factors involved. The practice of spending last month's income this month removes you from hope about money. (Hope is an emotional state that is questionably more comfortable than worry.) No longer will you be thinking, 'I hope the heating bill does not arrive until after pay day' or 'I hope this customer pays me soon so I can pay my rent.'

People who receive their income in irregular amounts find the Cash Flow Savings Account a useful method of leveling the hills and valleys. They do this by depositing their income into it and then paying themselves monthly from their Cash Flow Savings Account. This is a useful idea for anyone whose income varies widely from month to month and had been used effectively by architects, performing and creative artists of all kinds, consultants and authors.

LARGE PURCHASES SAVINGS ACCOUNT

The purpose of the Large Purchases Savings Account is to keep it empty. Deposit money into it regularly and withdraw the money for any purpose that you wish. Incidentally, this is the account that people with a single savings account usually have, however they have usually not given themselves permission to spend the money whenever they want to, so they end up beating themselves up when they make a withdrawal.

FINANCIAL INDEPENDENCE SAVINGS ACCOUNT

The purpose of the Financial Independence Savings Account is to become financially independent. Financial independence is having enough money coming in every month so that you can live in the style that you are accustomed to whether you work or not. Once you get in this position, your income will increase very rapidly because it is clear that you are working from choice, motivated by your desire to serve others. The Financial Independence Savings Account has two rules that go with it:

1. Never remove the principal.

2. Spend the interest regularly.

If you remove the principal you will become less financially independent each month. It is a good idea to ask your bank to mail you the interest from this account. The first interest check I received from my financial independence account was $3.63. At first, I was not very impressed about how financially independent I was, until I realized that a check for at least this much would be coming to me every quarter (four times per year) forever. I took the day off, cashed my check and spent the afternoon at the movies watching a double feature matinee allowing myself to feel what it felt like to be financially independent.

I call the income from my Financial Independence Savings Account "Eternal Regular Income" because it comes to me no matter what I do and will continue to do so forever.

MILLIONAIRE'S SAVINGS ACCOUNT

The purpose of the Millionaire's Savings Account is to become a Millionaire. The fastest way to become a millionaire is to master the FOUR LAWS OF WEALTH including the INVESTMENT LAW. The Millionaire's Savings Account is to accumulate cash to make investments. The rule it has is that you only withdraw money for the purpose of making investments.

ANNUAL INCOME SAVINGS ACCOUNT

The purpose of the Annual Income Savings Account is to accumulate an annual income so that you can take a year off. Although I recommend that everyone have an Annual Income Savings Account, this account is an especially important one for self-employed people who like their work so much that they never have time for vacations. There are several interesting ways that you can play with this account. One is to accumulate two day's income in it and then take a paid vacation day, paying yourself one day's income. You will have a day off and still have a day's income in the account when you return to work. Then accumulate four day's income and take two paid vacation days and so forth until you have graduated yourself to taking a year off.

Another way is to deposit 10% of your income into this account every pay period. Once per month withdraw 10% of the *balance* of this account and take a vacation for as much time as the money allows. This practice will cause both the balance in this account and your paid vacation time every month to increase.

Still a third way is to deposit 10% of your income into this account every pay period and allow it to accumulate until you have enough to take a year off. Mathematically it will take 6 to 7 years with interest to accumulate an annual income by saving 10% in this account. However you will probably discover that the impact of the growing balance upon your consciousness will at least cut this time in half.

TAXES SAVINGS ACCOUNT

The purpose the Taxes Saving Account is to accumulate cash so that you can pay your taxes when the time comes. If you are self-employed, it is a good idea to compute your tax liability monthly and to deposit enough cash into this account to cover it.

GENEROSITY SAVINGS ACCOUNT

The purpose of the Generosity Savings Account is to accumulate cash so that you can make large cash gifts to people. If you are already practicing generosity then you know that giving away cash is very different from giving other kinds of gifts. Giving away cash requires that you give up any ideas that you may have about what might be good for the recipient or what it is that they need to have. You will find that generosity will enable you to let go of your desire to control others and will increase your ability to express your love freely, instead of looking for something in return.

GETTING STARTED WITH SAVING

I suggest that all of your savings accounts be passbook accounts. If you travel a lot you may want your Cash Flow

Savings Account to be a statement savings account so that you can make frequent deposits by mail without waiting for the passbook to come back to you. According to personal preference, the accounts can all be at the same bank or all at different banks or any combination.

Here is a little trick that helped me to build the habit of regular savings when I was getting started. Pick one of the first four savings accounts listed at the beginning of this chapter. The trick is to have the Post Office remind you when it is time to save. You write out a check to the account that you have selected and mail it with the passbook to the bank. When the passbook comes back to you, mail in another deposit before you go to sleep that night. Another way of expressing this is that the passbook never sleeps at your house. Even if you can afford to deposit only a dollar when it is time to save, it is still worthwhile to do it. The regularity of the practice is the important thing here, not the size of the deposits. In fact, if you only deposit a dollar per week in each of your accounts, you will be doing more toward becoming a successful saver than if you put $200 once a month into one of them. The ultimate truth about saving is that saving has nothing to do with money; this is because regular saving is an affirmation that you have more money than you need and if you have more money than you need now then you will always have more money than you need, so you will never need the money that you are saving.

Affirmations about Saving
1. A part of all I earn is mine to keep.
2. Every day my income increases whether I am working, playing or sleeping.

A FINAL WORD OF CAUTION

Do not save for emergencies. If you do this then you are ordering your mind to create emergencies for yourself so you can spend the money that you have saved.

CHAPTER XI

The Investing Law

The INVESTING LAW can be thought of as a combination of the first three LAWS OF WEALTH. **THE INVESTING LAW** is spending the capital you saved with the purpose of earning a higher return than the savings and loan pays you.

In the next several chapters, I will discuss several common investment opportunities, provide you with ways to be successful regardless of what you invest in, and describe how to select the best investment opportunity for you. Contrary to popular opinion, it does not require a large sum of capital to become a successful investor. Many people who have attended my seminars have used the principles that I describe in this book to start their own successful business with an investment of less than $100.

BASIC INVESTING PRINCIPLES

Money follows the commands of your mind exactly. This is true regardless of the financial activity you engage in. It is true at your job, your business, in the stock market, in the gambling casino and at the race track. The basic affirmation about investing is: ALL MY INVESTMENTS ARE PROFITABLE. Your mind has the ability to make any percentage of your investments profitable, so why not 100%?

Eliminate worry from your investing. There are several ways to do this. Use your imagination to:
1. Find investments that you will not worry about.
2. Find creative ways to manage your investments so that your maximum loss is set at an amount that you will not worry about.

3. Use affirmations to accept your fear of loss and to use it to your benefit by letting it warn you of unsafe investments. It's better to miss a good investment because of fear of loss, than to make a bad one because of greed.

4. Invest only in things you love.

Manage your investment cash so that you can stay in the investment business forever. Surely this is long enough for anyone to learn to be a successful investor.

EXPLANATION OF BASIC INVESTING PRINCIPLES

If you have made some unsuccessful investments in the past, it is important to resolve any desire you may have left to blame other people or other forces outside yourself for your losses. As long as you are blaming your losses on the market, the stock broker, the real estate agent, your parents or a book you read, it is impossible for you to become a successful investor until you change these outside factors that you are blaming. Since you have little or no control over these outside factors, it is difficult to be a successful investor as long as you think that your results are affected by anything other than yourself. Taking responsibility for the results of your investing also facilitates learning.

Worrying about your investments will not increase your success. Even if you are successful with investments that you worry about, the ulcers and other physical tensions, will not make it worth it. The international economy offers a broad range of investment opportunities and will continue to do so. It is not necessary for you to master them all at once. Examples of investment opportunities:

Your Own Business—This can be anything that you can imagine.

Real Estate—Your own home, income property, real estate investment trusts, limited partnerships, vacation property, undeveloped property.

Securities—Government bonds, municipal bonds, corporate bonds, preferred stock, common stock, common stock op-

tions, commodities futures, currency speculation, commodities options, personal loans, second mortgages.
Personal Property—Art collections, rare coins, books and stamps, precious metals and gems, antique cars.

Certainly there are investment opportunities available every day that are not listed here. Each one of the investment opportunities that I have listed has a different risk profile and a different degree of liquidity.

Money is the commodity of investing. For this reason, it is important to learn to manage your investment capital in a way that you can stay in the investment business forever. The first principle is:

Always keep a portion of your investment capital in reserve.

This means you should never invest the entire balance of your Millionaire's Savings Account, so that you will always have cash to make investments. The second principle can be stated in affirmation form:

I always divide my profits into current expenses, financial independence, investments and reserves.

Let's say you invest $6000 in the stock market and realize a $2000 profit. When the sale is completed, you have $8000; the $6000 you started with and the $2000 in profit. You have already paid taxes on the $6000, but in most cases the $2000 is at least partially taxable. You can be certain of always having cash to invest if you return the $6000 of original capital to your Millionaire's Savings Account and divide the remaining $2000 (the profit) into four categories. The amount you put into each category is up to you.

1. Current expenses including taxes. Spend a portion of every profit you make so that your profits are not eternally reinvested and to reward yourself for being a good investor.

2. Financial Independence Savings Account. Deposit a portion into your Financial Independence Savings Account so that every profitable investment contributes to your Eternal Regular Income.

3. Take a portion of your profit and invest it in something else. This is the principle of diversification or spreading of investment risk to multiple investments. If you don't have an immediate available investment opportunity, you can place this portion of your profit into your Millionaire's Savings Account, until you find another investment opportunity.

4. Reserves. Deposit a portion of your profit into your Millionaire's Savings Account so that the capital you have to invest increases with every profitable investment.

OTHER FACTORS IN LEARNING TO INVEST

The fact that you have a sum of investment capital does not obligate you to make investments. I had a client once who hired me to teach her to invest the $500,000 she had just inherited. As she had no experience in investing, I suggested that she have two Millionaire's Savings Accounts and that she put $2000 in one of them and invest that until she had produced a success pattern. In the meantime, the remainder of the money remained intact in her second Millionaire's Savings Account.

It is also important to consider the kind of relationship that you enjoy having before you decide what to invest in. There is no reason that becoming a successful investor should require you to spend time with people whose company you don't like. You will have different relationships with different people if you decide to buy and manage an apartment building than if you decided to be an individual investor in the securities market.

Affirmations about Investing

1. Fear of loss is my friend.
2. I can learn from my mistakes.
3. My successful investments are good for the economy and everyone.
4. I use my capital and investments profits for the good of all.

CHAPTER XII

The Challenge and Benefits
of Your Own Business

It is not necessary to be an expert, have boundless confidence in yourself nor to have a six figure bank balance to start and succeed at you own business. Your own business does present challenges that are very different from those presented by a job.

Having your own successful business is the easiest way to build a success consciousness regarding money. You will find that the success consciousness that you build in your own business can easily be translated into success in real estate, the stock market or any other kind of investing that you want to do. I suggest that the best investment that you can make is to start a business that is so much fun that you don't care if you go broke. Your enthusiasm, coupled with applications of the principles in this book, make your success a foregone conclusion.

There are major differences between having a job and having your own business. Many of these are not obvious to people who have only had jobs and are thinking about starting their own business. The author acknowledges a strong preference for owning one's own business. The ability of the new business owner to adapt to these differences greatly determines the amount and rapidity of his or her success.

Having a job is fine. A job is an excellent way to learn a marketable skill, to learn to work with others and to learn to manage your time and your money. If you think about it this way, you can use your job as a stepping stone to your own business. It is the individual businessperson that is the foundation of any prosperous economy. A country is not made great by employees, who follow instructions; but rather by the individual business people who are willing to take initiative and responsibility. The vast majority of new jobs in the U.S. in the 1980's have been provided by companies with sales of less than $20 million annually. The talented leadership of the Fortune 500 companies spends its time either trying to buy someone else's company or preventing their own from being taken over. New and small businesses are the potential for the future growth and stability in our economy.

Quitting your job is bound to be scary. While you can dream and even plan with great precision, thinking about quitting that job will likely feel like leaping from a high diving board, no matter how well prepared you are. If you wait for the fear to go away, you'll never do it. The realization that I was the one who had created the job I had, and that I could create another one just as satisfying gave me the courage to leap.

METHOD OF COMPENSATION

In a job your compensation is based on the time you put in. The unit of time measurement may be as short as one hour or as long as a year. Your employer accepts the challenge of using his supervisory ability and authority to ensure that he receives service from you that is of greater value than your pay. In your own business you are paid directly for the service you provide and you must bear the supervisory challenge yourself. This factor aids you in increasing your income by starting your own business, because, all things equal, you can keep the profit that your employer had been receiving from your services. Since you must formulate and follow your own instructions, self-discipline is required in your own business.

AMOUNT OF COMPENSATION

A survey of American millionaires that was published by USA Today reported that 70% of American millionaires work for themselves, 20% are retired and 10% work for someone else. Clearly the precision of such surveys is always open to question; however, it is pretty easy to figure out that your chances of becoming a millionaire working for someone else are very slim. In a job your income depends more on the salary policy of your company than on the quantity and quality of your work. In your own business, your income depends on the quality and quantity of your output, rather than on the amount of time or energy that you put in. The ability to distinguish between effort and results is required in your own business.

FINANCIAL SECURITY

With a job you have placed a lid on your income in exchange for an illusion of financial security. Only you can decide if you have made a wise choice. The illusion that a job provides financial security is well developed in most people's minds as a result of parental example. The involuntary destruction of this illusion is a painful and devastating experience for people put out of work by business takeovers and re-organizations and plant closings. With your own business, your financial security does not depend on anyone else. You become the daily creator of your financial security based on your ability to attract and your willingness to serve your customers. Courage is required in your own business.

EMOTIONAL CONTENT

A person with his own business confronts a variety of emotional conflicts that an employee rarely or never experiences. Fear of loss is potentially more intense, because the self-employed person pays for his mistakes and poor judgments with his own money. Despite the fact that a job provides only illusionary security, not having one tends to activate previously suppressed issues about survival, at least at first. Fear of failure is more intense because the self-employed person puts his reputation about his ability on the line with each new customer. Additionally, the independent business person confronts his fear of rejection with each potential customer. Knowing how to resolve internal emotional conflicts is required in your own business.

FORMULATION OF GOALS

At a job the goals and plans that direct your activities and thinking are defined for you, or in some cases you participate in their formulation in some kind of group process. In your own business, it is up to you to formulate your own goals and plans. There is nothing to stop you from defining any goal you choose and accomplishing it in any way you see fit. A clear sense of direction is required in your own business.

TIME FOCUS

In some jobs, you can show up for work, do what needs to be done and go home and forget about it. In your own business all of the planning rests with you. Generally, a person in his own business needs to be able to think further into the future than a person in a job. Clarity of abstract thought is required in your own business.

MANAGING OTHERS

The people who start their own business tend to be those with a high value on independence and self-reliance. These character traits usually accompany ideas like, "I can do everything myself." Now it is fine to think that you can do everything yourself; however, it is unwise to think that it is necessary to prove this. If you think that you must do everything yourself, then you will have difficulty expanding your business beyond a one person operation. This is an instance where the qualities that motivate you to take the risk of starting your own business are not necessarily the ones that enable you to succeed at it. Clearly at first, you neither need nor can afford even one full time employee. However, if you wait until you can afford a full time employee before you get help, you will be so busy that it is unlikely that you will get yourself to a position where you can afford one. If you generate $25 per hour in your business and your accountant quotes $25 per hour for his or her services, then you can actually easily afford the accountant in small amounts. This is because hiring the accountant means your accounting will be done better, in less time than you would have spent doing it (while giving up $25 per hour income from your business) and, assuming that you prefer your own business to accounting, you will enjoy yourself more. As your business grows, develop the ability to identify the tasks that you could delegate to others and use part time employees or hire sub-contractors at first. The ability to motivate, acknowledge and manage others is essential in your own business.

BOOKKEEPING

In a job, your employer tells you (and the IRS) how much you were paid during the year and (although increasingly complicated), filing a tax return is reasonably straightforward. In your own business, it is up to you to keep the books, or hire someone else to do it for you; not only to keep the IRS happy, but more importantly so that you can use the information in your profit and loss statement and balance sheet to manage your business intelligently. A knowledge of accounting is required in your own business.

INITIATIVE

In your own business, there is no one to tell you what to do. Most of us were brought up surrounded by authority figures, some of whom even got paid for telling us what to do. While it is definitely a good idea to be able to recognize good advice when you hear it, in your own business, you step out on your own, without anyone to tell you what to do. You must be able to recognize opportunities that come along and act on them.

INDEPENDENCE

In a job, hours, location, work methods and sometimes lots of minute details are already defined for you. In your own business, it is up to you to set your own schedule and work methods. When you succeed, no one else takes the credit, but there is no one to blame either. A sense of responsibility is required in your own business.

THE CHALLENGE OF SALES

In a job you sold your employer on your abilities when you were hired and continue to do so each workday, despite the fact that you may not think about it that way. In your own business, do not expect to hang out your sign and make change for the onrush of customers. You take the initiative to find the people who can use what you are offering and to convince them of the benefits of your service or product. Fears about confronting the challenge of sales stops more people from starting their own business than any other. For this reason, the entire next chapter is devoted to learning how to sell.

WINNING IN YOUR OWN BUSINESS

It is a good idea to open a business checking account to handle your buy and sell business. Use the money in this account to buy inventory and deposit the proceeds of your sales into it. This way it doesn't matter how sloppy your accounting system is, you will be able to see your success. Also it is important to pay yourself a salary, by dividing your profits into the four categories explained in the previous chapter. Several years ago I began buying and selling self-improvement audio cassette tapes. At first I bought my inventory with money in my personal checking account and deposited the money from the sales into the same place. I sold several dozen tapes before I realized that I couldn't find the profit I was making. I knew I must be making a profit, but I couldn't find it because it was disguised by the other transactions in my personal checking account. When I opened a business checking account, just for the tapes, the profit became obvious because the balance in that account kept increasing and I always had a supply of tapes to sell. At that point I had more ideas about how to expand the business than I had money to expand it so I went for several months without paying myself a salary. I found that my sales declined. I decided to pay myself a salary of $10 per month whether the business could afford it or not and the sales began increasing again. If you run your business from the point of view that you are the servant and the business is the master, you are just making it difficult for yourself. You created the business to serve you, and it will serve you if you take the point of view of master.

BUSINESS POLICIES YOU CAN WIN WITH

Getting started. When you start in a service business an easy way to create an abundance of clients is to give away your service at the beginning until you have more clients than you can handle or until people force you to accept money. If you don't like your business well enough to give away your services, this may be an indication to you that you are in the wrong business. When you have an abundance of clients, it is a good idea to continue to give away a portion of your services, even if you have to refuse the money.

Make a schedule. Create a personal schedule for yourself of when you want to work with time slots for each client. This way you will be certain of working when you want to. Whenever you have an empty time slot, spend the time figuring out what you could do to fill it.

MONEY BACK GUARANTEE

In any business, it is always wise to offer a money back guarantee. This guarantee is for your benefit, not for the benefit of your clients. When you have a money back guarantee, you will never have to accept money from people unless they are willing to give it to you. This policy will increase your certainty of the willingness of others to prosper you.

ALL PRICES ARE NEGOTIABLE

A willingness to negotiate prices and to accept payment in products and services from your clients will not only expand your business, but will give you increased opportunities to practice your negotiating skills.

Your own business can be thought of as a Money Machine. People with well developed prosperity consciousness find it easy to create a new money machine every day if they want to. With a prosperity consciousness, it does not matter whether your money machine is well oiled or not; you can turn the crank whenever you want to and money will pour out. A prosperity consciousness is the key, however, as many of the businesses that file bankruptcy are well-oiled machines run according to the most scientific, modern business practices except there was no prosperity consciousness.

Chapter XIII

THE ART OF SALES(WO)MANSHIP
OR WHY IT IS ESSENTIAL TO LEARN TO SELL

Your income depends on your sales ability. This happens to be so whether or not you have thought about it this way before. Most people are accustomed to receiving their income from a job. Even in the instance of a job, you sold your services to your employer when you were hired and continue to do so by the performance of your work. Every transaction is an exchange of goods and/or services between a buyer and a seller. In every instance, the buyer and the seller both believe that they are getting more than they are giving; otherwise, no transaction would occur. The process of convincing a buyer that the goods and/or services offered are worth more than the asking price is known as selling. No transactions occur without selling.

Unfortunately, there is virtually no training about selling offered in the formal educational system. This may be caused by the fact that the vast majority of school teachers are government employees and governments have traditionally relied on coercion, rather than good salesmanship, to provide revenue. This problem could be rectified by making mastery of sales a requirement for graduating grammar school. Such a simple modification to our educational system has the potential for putting more people to work and more potential for reducing taxpayer cost of welfare programs than anything else I can think of. Whatever the cause of this glaring omission in our educational system, selling is something that you'll have to teach yourself. It's a lot easier than you think. Learning to sell is also far more valuable than you may have thought. Fear

103

about selling stops more people who desire to start a business of their own than anything else.

MYTHS ABOUT SELLING

Myth: Salespeople are in it for the money.

Reality: Some are. The ones who succeed and last are motivated by service. At any rate, your own motivation is up to you.

Myth: Selling is a dead end job.

Reality: All income results from sales. Once you master selling, you can use your skill to sell whatever you choose. Additionally, you can make money anywhere in the world.

Myth: Salespeople are dishonest;

Reality: Some are. If you read the paper, you know that some politicians, ministers, police officials, stock brokers and corporate executives are dishonest, too.

Myth: Women can't make it in sales.

Reality: There are higher percentages of women in sales than in most professional occupations. In sales, where performance is more measurable than many occupations, the income gap between men and women is the smallest.

Myth: It is more important that people like me than that they buy from me.

Reality: People either like you or they don't. It's not up to you. You can put on an act to influence them to like you, but that is not worth the effort because you have to keep doing it.

Myth: People must like me for them to buy from me.

Reality: Surely you have made purchases from people that you didn't like. People's opinions about us are really about them. I think it is at least mildly humorous that we live with ourselves for decades with a limited understanding of our behavior and mental processes; but nevertheless, think we can figure everything about someone else in the first two minutes.

HERE IS HOW ANYONE CAN LEARN TO SELL.

Look around your house, your car, your office and your purse and find a possession with the following characteristics:

1. **A product with a retail price of $1-$10.**
2. **Easily available in wholesale quantity and at wholesale prices.**
3. **Something you did not make yourself.**
4. **Something that you delight in owning.**

EXPLANATION OF SUGGESTED CHARACTERISTICS:

1. A product with a retail price of $1-$10.

At the beginning, a product is easier to sell than a service. Your customer can examine the product that you are offering to discover if it is something that he wants; with a service however, the customer doesn't really know what he is getting until after he has agreed to accept delivery. This makes the selling task somewhat more complex for services. By starting with an inexpensive product, you minimize the size of your investment, maximize your potential market and have a product that you can carry with you. Clearly, it would be foolish to invest your entire life savings in inventory, if you have not yet mastered selling. At first, it is important to gain experience quickly. Almost everyone is a potential customer for a $1-$10 item, because almost everyone has this much money at hand and is accustomed to spending this amount of money frequently. People spend multiple thousands of dollars in a single transaction much less frequently. It is not necessary to move to a higher priced item to increase your sales. McDonalds is an example of a commercially successful enterprise that sells nothing that even comes close to $10 in selling price. The publishing company which I started in 1979 could be characterized as an embodiment of the $1-$10 idea, resulting in sales of thousands of books every year.

There are many ways to find a product to sell. Consult your Yellow Pages, the manufacturer or the retailer where you bought it to find out how to obtain a supply at wholesale prices. Many people have used this book as a product for learning to sell. Not only does it meet all the requirements for a product to learn with; if you have difficulty with selling your supply you can sit down and read the book to help you out. To obtain a supply of this book, check or money order (US funds preferred) VISA and Mastercard accepted also, to:

Vivation Publishing Co.
PO Box 8269
Cincinnati, OH 45208 USA

Number of Copies	Price
5	$30
10	$55
20	$90

Prices include surface delivery anywhere throughout the world.

2. Easily available in wholesale quantity and at wholesale prices.

Once you have sold your inventory, you want to be able to replenish it easily and quickly. If you can't replenish your inventory quickly, you will lose sales to people who approach you wanting to buy your product which temporarily you cannot deliver. Being out of stock is bad for business. Buying at wholesale prices and selling at retail is a natural and normal thing to do. Wholesale prices (cheaper by the dozen) are based on the supposition by the supplier that if you buy in quantity, then it costs the supplier less selling expense per unit to deliver the product to you, because you as the customer are doing the selling. Additionally the supplier anticipates that you will return for more after you have sold your first batch. The mark up of the retail price above the wholesale price is your reward for your selling efforts. All of this may seem quite unusual to someone who has not managed his own business; however, the system of wholesale and retail prices is clearly more common than you may think—there would be no shopping centers, car dealerships, or department stores without it.

3. Something you did not make yourself.

It is substantially more difficult to sell a product that you made yourself. Selling a product of your own creation is more emotionally confronting and rejection seems tougher to take. In 1976, I started a business selling self-improvement books and audio cassettes. I lived in the Boston area at the time and within a year or so, I was serving customers throughout the East Coast of the United States. In 1979, I published the first edition of this book. The emotional content of selling it was far more intense than selling books that other people had written. I can remember standing in bookstores while the book buyer looked through my book, deciding whether to purchase a supply, and thinking that it would probably be less embarrassing for me to remove all my clothing than to have my book examined like this. This emotional intensity is a serious problem for anyone in the performing or creative arts. Poor salesmanship is the primary cause of the starving artist syndrome. For this reason, actors, musicians and writers, anyone in the creative or performing arts and anyone else who offers a service stands to benefit promptly from the skill gained by selling a product that is not of their own creation.

4. Something that you delight in owning.

By choosing a product that you delight in owning, you make it easy for yourself to say good things about it. Just allow your enthusiasm for what you have to come forth. With a product that you love, it is not necessary to make up lies about it in order to sell.

Offer your product to people that you know and meet. Obviously, at first the income that you receive from this activity will be a whole lot less than you would receive from all but the lowest paying job; however, at first, the learning is more important than the income. The same skills are required to sell a $100,000 item and a $5 item. This has been proven repeatedly by real estate sales people who double their real estate commissions as a result of the practice gained by selling their favorite book.

HOW TO SELL

Like most skills, the sales process breaks down into a few simple steps that anyone can learn.

1. **Initial Contact**
2. **Qualification**
3. **Presentation**
4. **Close**
5. **Re-Close**

1. Initial Contact: Selling clearly involves communication. Getting the attention of your audience, whether one person or thousands, is the first step. If at any point later in the process, the seller loses the attention of the customer, then it is necessary to regain it before proceeding.

2. Qualification: Not everyone wants the product or service that you offer. In a certain sense, selling is like a treasure hunt where buyers who accept your offer are the treasure. You can serve more people and have greater success by identifying interested buyers as quickly as possible. The most straightforward way to do this is to request an acknowledgement of interest from the prospective buyer. Without an acknowledgement of at least mild interest by the prospective customer all concerned are wasting time by continuing. It is important to remember that some customers will keep listening to what you have to say, even after they have said they are not interested. An example of the axiom, "Actions speak louder than words." Learn to ask lots of questions during the Qualification phase. Some of the questions I have asked in selling books are: "Do you like to read?", "What have you been reading?", "Are you interested in learning how to increase your income?"

3. Presentation: The purpose of the Presentation is to convey information to the customer regarding the characteristics and benefits of the product or service offered. When selling a product, it is a good idea to hand one to your customer for examination.

4. Close: To Close the sale, the seller provides the customer with buying instructions. This is done by letting the customer know what action is required to make the purchase. This is by far the most emotionally activating portion of the selling process and could be called The Most Embarrassing Moment. Without presenting your Close, i.e. asking for payment; you are not really selling, you are just talking.

5. Re-Close: If the customer has not followed the buying instructions, the final step is to respond to customer considerations. Considerations are about one of three things: 1) Time, 2) Money or 3) Something else. If you hear considerations about time or about money, then immediately return to step 3 and present benefits. Regarding customer reservations about time, you, as the sales(wo)man cannot manage someone else's time. When a customer says "I don't have time (to attend concerts)", for example; he means that you have not convinced him that the concert ticket you are offering is more valuable than the use that he has planned for the time involved or you have not convinced him that the concert is a better use of his time than some other opportunity that may come his way between now and then. It is foolish and unproductive to argue with your customer about how he wants to spend his time, so for that reason, return to emphasizing important benefits, if you hear time considerations.

Also, if you are hearing considerations about money, it is equally foolish and unproductive to argue with your customer about what he can afford. If your customer says, "I can't afford it", he usually means "You have not convinced me that what you are offering is more valuable than what it costs" or "You haven't convinced me that what you are offering is more valuable than what I am now buying with my money (or plan to buy with my money)." Almost anyone who can afford a moderately priced apartment or house can afford a Rolls Royce, although few people think about it this way. If you have a house or apartment and not a Rolls, then you could move out of your current lodging and begin living in your Rolls Royce; using the income you are now paying for housing to make payments on the Rolls. Therefore, the reason that most people have apartments instead of Rolls Royces is not that they can't afford the Rolls; but rather that they place a higher value on the housing than on a luxury motor car. For this reason, the best thing to do when you are hearing considerations about money is to re-emphasize the benefits of what you are offering. Another way to say this is that your customer and everyone else spends his time and money in the way that they believe most supports their own values. For this reason, you want to ask questions during the Qualification Phase to learn enough about your customer's values so that you know which benefits to emphasize during the Presentation Phase. In some instances, time and money considerations are habitual methods of saying NO. If you hear them a lot, work on improving your ability to find out what interests the customer in the Qualification section. If you are hearing considerations about anything else (color, size, delivery, etc.), then simply answer the questions honestly and present the buying instructions again.

THE MISSION OF THE SALES(WO)MAN

The mission of the sales(wo)man is to provide the prospective buyer with an opportunity. The customer is the one who exercises his choice to accept or decline. The mission of the sales(wo)man, then, is to aid the customer in making a choice. This is done by continuing the communication until the customer accepts or declines the offer. Another way to say this is that the mission of the sales(wo)man is to continue the discussion until the customer says yes, no or refuses to discuss the issue further.

COMMON MISTAKES OF NEW SALESPEOPLE

Refer to this section frequently to improve your selling techniques.

Focusing on the money you will get instead of the benefit that you will deliver. It is very difficult to sell when you are broke. The practice of carrying a $100 bill as described earlier will serve to focus your attention on the benefit you are delivering the customer. By offering your product to the customer, you are providing him with an opportunity that he may not get without you. In this way you serve your customer whether he buys or not. If your attention is focused on the money that you will make, then it is likely that your customer will feel like you are pushing him.

NERVOUSNESS RESULTS IN TOO MUCH TALK AND TOO LITTLE LISTENING.

An excellent way to avoid this problem is to ask lots of questions and listen carefully to your customer. The purpose of the questions is to find out which benefits of your product or service interest your customer most. The customer who says "I don't know" is further from buying than one who says "No". This is because the "I don't know" customer has not considered your offer fully enough to make up his mind and/or to express what is on his mind. It is impossible for the customer to buy with his mind in "I don't know." Although it may sound strange, you have a greater possibility of making a sale to a customer who is saying "No" than to one who is saying "I don't know." This is because when a person makes a choice, he has a chance to see how his decision feels to him. In other words, he can check out the sensations in his body and know whether he has made the right decision for him. The "I don't know" person receives no such information from his body because "I don't know" feels the same, no matter what is being considered. When the customer says "I don't know", it is a good idea to return to a presentation of some of the benefits that you think are most important to him. Additionally, it is possible to point out to the customer that by saying "I don't know", he is depriving himself of your product or service.

STRESSING PRICE OVER BENEFITS.

As mentioned in the Chapter about the Spending Law, all prices are arbitrary. It does not necessarily follow that it is to the benefit of the sales(wo)man to cave in on price to make the sale. Price concessions are almost always a sign of poor salesmanship. Set fair prices and the time that you spend convincing your customer that what you have is worth what you are asking will be time well spent.

FEAR OF REJECTION.

The sales(wo)man confronts his fear of rejection with every customer. "NO" is a little word, but generates totally disproportionate anxiety. Some of the customers that you contact will say "NO", no matter how good you are. "NO" does not mean that you are no good, that you are a failure, that there is something wrong with you or anything like that. If you think "NO" means any of these things, you'll never even get started with selling. It is a good idea for you to make a new definition of "NO" that does not disable your sales efforts. My favorite is "NO" means, I decline your offer, I love you, I admire you, I respect you and I am open to future offers.

Without an effective humorous way of dealing with fear of rejection, new sales people will tend to make other common mistakes which are: wasting too much time on customers who do not buy, failing to offer the customer a chance to buy and lack of emotional honesty.

As mentioned earlier, it is unlikely that everyone you contact will buy what you are offering. If you have difficulty accepting "NO" for an answer, you'll waste too much time talking to those people who will not buy, but who are too polite to ask you to stop talking.

Often new sales people do great jobs on Initial Contact, Qualification and Presentation but fail to present a Close, thereby failing to offer the customer the opportunity to complete the transaction. Unless you present a Close, you are not selling, you're merely having a conversation. In other words, unless you say something equivalent to "This item costs five dollars. If you want one, please give me five dollars"; you are simply having a pleasant conversation.

For other new sales people, their fear of rejection causes them to give up too easily. They give up at the first hint of resistance from the customer. I am not suggesting that you badger customers to buy after they have said no repeatedly; however, it is important to remember that many people say no as a habit whenever they are first offered something new.

No matter how experienced you are at selling, it hurts when your customer says no. New sales people who find it difficult to deal with rejection may adopt the attitude, "It doesn't matter if that customer didn't buy. There are plenty of customers around." Clearly the part about plenty of customers is accurate; however, you will be a much more effective sales(wo)man if you acknowledge your disappointment at your customer's decision by saying something like, "I am disappointed that you didn't buy, because I know that you would enjoy having (whatever you are offering). Thanks for listening." The purpose here is not to influence the buying decision, but rather to preserve emotional integrity for the sales(wo)man.

EXCESSIVE POLITENESS.

It is fine to be polite. If you are not experienced at sales, it is possible that your behavior is governed by rules about manners that are far stricter than necessary for an effective sales(wo)man. If your parents encouraged you to sit down and be quiet rather than ask for what you want, then even considering selling something may seem like a violation of manners and an imposition upon others. When selling this book I have said, "You have told me about the problems that you have with money and yet you are telling me that you don't want to spend the money on a book that will help you solve them. Is this really what you mean?" A statement like this may not meet the politeness standards of some people; however it is likely that you will discover that your customers are far less easily offended than were your parents, who are the people who laid down the first rules about politeness. If you do offend someone, apologize immediately for your over-zealousness.

THE BELIEF THAT SELLING IS WEIRD.

When you are selling, you are simply asking people to spend money. Everyone likes to spend money and does so regularly. There is nothing weird about it, except that it may be new to you.

THE IDEA THAT SELLING IS BENEATH YOU IS A VERY EXPENSIVE SELF-DELUSION.

You are selling all the time. You sell your services to your employer, you sell your ideas and opinions to your friends, your family and associates regularly. Sales is as noble a profession as any, despite the fact that some people prefer to maintain the delusion that selling is beneath them, even at the cost of staying at a dead end job.

Almost anyone can earn the income he wants by mastering sales. Neither education, social position nor wealth are required to start and to succeed at it. Even a bed ridden person can serve many people and reap great rewards through telephone sales.

Learning to sell is your gateway to a whole new world of financial success. Get started today and read over this chapter frequently to accelerate your development.

Affirmations about Selling

1. I am an attractive, loving person with money.
2. I am attracting loving people with money to me and they are attracting me.
3. I receive assistance and co-operation from those people everywhere necessary for me to achieve my desired result.
4. My customers like me.
5. I like my customers.
6. My customers buy from me whether they like me or not.
7. I sell products and services that benefit everyone.
8. I am clever enough to get rejected.
9. If people say no, I never take it personally.
10. The more I sell, the easier it becomes; and the easier it becomes the more I sell.
11. Sales is a fine profession for me.
12. I love everything about selling.
13. NO means I decline your offer, I love you, I admire you, I respect you and I am open to future offers.
14. I forgive all those people who ever told me to sit down and shut up.
15. Now I can appreciate the humor in worrying about other people's opinions of me.

CHAPTER XIV

Investing in Real Estate

If you can afford rent you can afford to own your own home. Rent is the worst investment you can make. Rent buys you shelter for thirty days, at which point you have to pay it again, with nothing but a canceled check to show for it.

There are at least three characteristics about real estate that make it easy for you to own your own home. There are: the nature of the expenses of owning real estate, the ease of financing because of the willingness of financial institutions to make loans backed by real estate, and the flexibility of real estate.

THE NATURE OF REAL ESTATE EXPENSES

The primary expenses of owning real estate are principal, interest and taxes. Principal is the money you repay to the mortgage holder. Since these payments reduce your indebtedness, they are akin to savings. Interest and real estate taxes are deductible on your federal and state income tax. Therefore, depending on your tax rate, the monthly payments that you make for principle, interest and taxes can be 20-100% higher than your present rent and you will be spending the same amount of money for shelter. This is because the money you save on taxes.

EASE OF FINANCING

Whether you have cash for the downpayment or not, it is easy to finance the purchase of a piece of real estate that you want to own. In my consulting with real estate buyers, I have devised several ways to buy real estate without cash. The basic principle is—if you don't have cash or you don't have credit, then use someone else's. With this general principle in mind, you can devise other ways to buy real estate without cash, or use one of these if you want to.

SECOND MORTGAGE

A second mortgage will enable you to borrow the down payment from the seller or another person or from an institution. I have found that asking the seller to take a second mortgage works especially well when the seller has owned the property for a long time. This is because the seller in this case usually has a relatively small balance remaining on the mortgage, reducing the cash required for the seller to complete the transaction. Let's say the purchase price is $40,000 and the seller has a balance of $6,000 remaining on their mortgage and that you, as buyer, are able to obtain 80% financing from the bank. In this case, the buyer would ask the seller to finance the remaining 20% of the purchase price or $8,000. The seller receives the $32,000 in cash that you borrowed from the bank, uses $6,000 of it to pay the balance on the existing mortgage and has $26,000 to put down on his or her next house, plus a regular monthly income from you as you make the payments on the second mortgage.

LEASE WITH AN OPTION TO BUY

A lease with an option to buy will let you have a portion of your rent go towards the down payment of the house you are renting. After you have lived there long enough to have paid enough rent to accumulate a down payment, you can then go to the bank for a mortgage loan to finance the rest. The benefits of this agreement to the seller are having a tenant that likes the house well enough to want to buy it. This will eliminate any problems of vacancies and ensure that the owner has a tenant who will love and care for the property.

SALE/LEASEBACK

Sale/leaseback is a good arrangement when the seller is either unwilling or unable to accept one of the first two approaches. In sale/leaseback you find a third party who is willing to buy the house with conventional terms from the seller and then lease the house to you with an option to buy. For the third party investor, you have the best of all real estate opportunities because he or she can determine the profit that will be made from the entire transaction up to completion when you buy the house, before any money is invested. Additionally the third party investor is assured of having a tenant that will take care of the property and has a very low likelihood of moving out.

LAND CONTRACT

A land contract works especially well when a regular monthly income is more important to the seller than a lump sum of cash. For example, the seller may own two homes, one of which is being sold. Under a land contract the seller finances the entire amount of the purchase price, which the buyer repays in monthly payments. Let's say that the seller has a house which he or she bought several years ago for $40,000 by making a $10,000 down payment and by giving the bank a mortgage for the remaining $30,000. The house is now for sale for $60,000. As the buyer you give the seller a mortgage for $60,000 and you move in. The seller must continue to make the monthly payments on the $30,000, but assuming approximately equal interest rates and length of mortgage, the payments you make each month to the seller on the $60,000 mortgage will be approximately twice the payment the seller has on the $30,000 mortgage.

INCOME TAX IMPLICATIONS OF BUYING REAL ESTATE WITHOUT CASH

If you research the income tax implications to the seller of any of the transactions I have described, you will discover that the seller usually receives a tax saving compared to selling the real estate by conventional means, and that ultimately the government finances the down payment for the buyer. Every federal administration since Truman has been encouraging

Americans to own their own home. It's time to take them up on it.

NEGOTIATING THE TRANSACTION

Frequently in real estate transactions, price is the only variable that is discussed. There are only three things that matter in real estate transactions: 1) terms, 2) terms, and 3) terms. Consider for a moment that with the right terms you could buy the World Trade Center in New York City (assuming you want it). In buying real estate without cash it will be necessary for you to negotiate directly with the seller. The real estate agent can be of assistance to you in your negotiations so it is a good idea to ask him or her to be present at the meetings you have with the seller. As in all negotiations, the way to make the best transaction for all concerned, is to find out what the other person really wants and then figure out the best way for you to give it to them.

THE FLEXIBILITY OF REAL ESTATE

Real Estate is the simplest investment you can make. After all, it is just a bunch of dirt, sticks and rocks. In the 1870's when gold was plentiful at the height of the gold rush in California, the price of gold was $16 per ounce. Now over 100 years later it sells for about $470 per ounce. This is an average annual increase of about 3% per year. In my experience, it is almost impossible to do worse than that in real estate. The Basic Law of Real Estate Value is that the value of real estate is determined by the income that it produces, be that income psychic or financial. The income that a piece of real estate produces is largely the result of what the real estate is used for. So, the way to increase the value of your real estate is to increase the quality of ideas that you have about what it can be used for.

An interesting application of this idea can be observed in the introduction of breakfast foods at McDonald's Restaurants. Before the introduction of breakfasts, someone at McDonald's was smart enough to see that there were pieces of real estate all over the country that were being used to sell hamburgers, but that there are only a few people around who have trained themselves to enjoy hamburgers at 7 a.m. The introduction of breakfast foods was a way to increase the cash flow of the company without any additional investment in real estate.

After checking local zoning laws, it is likely that that can think of lots of ways to generate additional income from any piece of real estate.

CHAPTER XV

Investing in Securities

Although this chapter is primarily devoted to investing in common stock, there is nothing to stop you from applying the principles in this book to any kind of securities trading.

I first became aware of the stock market at age nineteen. At first I was overwhelmed by the amount of knowledge it seemed to require. In fact, the reason that many people are unsuccessful in the stock market is because they immerse themselves in such an incomprehensible mass of unrelated data that it is almost impossible to sort out the relevant from the irrelevant. The first approach I came up with was to devote my attention and my investing to twenty stocks that I watched closely. Some of them I never invested in, but my attention was focused and I agreed with myself to ignore all information about other stocks no matter how insistent the person was who was trying to give me the information. I was pretty successful with my twenty stock mini-market for two reasons— first my attention was focused and most importantly I was careful to accept responsibility for my results. Since I had selected which stocks I wanted to follow and since I was acting as my own investment advisor, there was no one I could blame except myself when I had a trade that resulted in a loss. Whenever I had a trade that produced a loss I would sit down and examine myself until I found the thought or thoughts that caused it. I knew that if I was only a good enough investor to buy losers, I had better do something to become a better investor before I bought my next stock, or there was no reason that the next one would be anything other than another loser. This is a very interesting way to learn about yourself. If nothing else, you will find out what it means to be certain about your investments.

THE LITTLE OLD LADY APPROACH

Little Old Ladies are very successful in the stock market. Frequent surveys of the ownership of the stock traded on the New York Stock Exchange indicated that many of the shares are owned by females and that the average age of these people is high. So it seems that they must be doing something right. It is paradoxical that the reason that they are so successful is that they do not invest for capital appreciation, instead they invest primarily for income. With my twenty stock mini-market, I had picked the stocks I wanted to watch pretty much arbitrarily and without a system. The Little Old Lady Approach uses three things as qualifying factors for stock selection—these are yield, fundamentals and potential. Before further description, it is necessary to explain these three principles. All the information that you need for this can be found on the Standard and Poor's sheet for the stock in question. These sheets are available at most brokerage offices and public libraries.

YIELD

Yield is the ratio between the annual cash dividend per share paid by a stock and the current market price. The annual cash dividend per share is the money paid by the company directly to the shareholders. The annual dividend is usually paid in four equal payments at three month intervals. The current market price is the price of the stock as of the last trade on the exchange. So, if a company pays an annual cash dividend of $3.20 per share and if the current market price is $40 per share, then the yield is $3.20 divided by $40 or 8%. An important characteristic of the yield is that it varies inversely with the price, so as the price of the stock increases, the yield decreases and vice versa. For example if the price of the stock I just described dropped to $32 per share, the yield would become $3.20 divided by $32 or 10%.

FUNDAMENTALS

Fundamentals are the inherent strength of the company. Especially at the beginning, it is best to invest in companies that have sales in the hundreds of millions of dollars, that show a pattern of increasing sales every year for the last five years and that show a pattern of increasing profits and increasing dividends.

POTENTIAL

Potential will give you an indication of how high you can expect the price of the stock to go. Potential has two dimensions—there is time potential and price potential. To determine the price potential, look at the highest price that the stock has ever sold at. The price potential is the difference between the current price and the highest price expressed as a percentage of the current price. For example, if you have a stock with a current price of $20 per share and an all time high $45 per share, then the difference between the current price and the all time high is $25 and the potential is $25 divided by $20 or 125%. The time potential is how long ago the stock sold at its all time high.

STOCK SELECTION

Start with stocks on the New York Stock Exchange with yields in excess of 7% and examine their fundamentals and potential. You will probably find that a lot of the companies with high yielding stocks are utilities. The major differences between utilities and other companies is that the profits of utilities are regulated by a Government agency. You will be most certain of stocks with strong fundamentals, high price potentials and short time potentials. If the all time high occurred more than five years ago, it is wise to compute another price potential and time potential based on a more recent peak in price.

WHY THE LITTLE OLD LADY APPROACH WORKS

This works for two reasons; one is that Little Old Ladies are interested in income, not in capital appreciation and the other is that companies that pay dividends consider it important to maintain a stable dividend pattern. For this reason, they are careful to increase the dividend only when they are pretty sure that they can maintain it over the years. After all, if they cut the dividend, they incur the disappointment of those little old ladies who are the shareholders and who would sell their stock if that happened. Although dividend cuts are not unknown, companies with sales in the hundreds of millions of dollars typically have sufficient resources to borrow money to pay dividends, in the event of a temporary slackening in business.

This means that when the price of stocks is high then simultaneously their yields are low. Little Old Ladies look at their portfolios and see that it is yielding 4%. "I can do better than this at the savings and loan," they say, so they sell their stock and put the money in the bank while at the same time enjoying an increase in income. More desire to sell than to buy will cause the prices of stocks to go down every time. As the prices drop, the yields increase. Any Little Old Lady worth her salt would not leave her money in the bank at 5% when there are good stocks to be had that are yielding 8%. So, the money flows out of the savings and loans and back into the stock market, driving the prices back up again. As you can see Little Old Ladies represent the world's largest unorganized mutual fund.

Do not be surprised if hot shot brokers tell you that this approach is too slow, that it will take forever to get rich this way. I don't know many hot shot brokers that support themselves year after year solely on their investment income. Little Old Ladies do it all the time.

MARKET STRATEGY TO AVOID ULCERS

We will assume that you purchased 100 shares of a stock at a price of $40 per share and with a dividend of $3.20 per share. This means that the yield is 8%. The yield acts as a protection against drops in price. If the price drops to $35 per share, then the yield increase to 9%. If your stock was a good buy when it yielded 8% then it is now a better buy and more people will want to buy it. At this point, you should consider buying more; either using the part of the reserve you left in your Millionaire's Savings Account or if you want to be daring you can buy more by borrowing on the margin from your broker.

As the price increases, I suggest you use stop sell orders so you don't have to worry about your portfolio. A stop sell order is an order to your broker to sell your stock at a specified price. When the price gets to $50 per share, you might want to put in a stop sell order at $46-1/2 per share. This means that you have locked in your profit, because if the price ever drops to $46-1/2 per share, your broker will automatically sell it for you. As the price continues to increase, it is a good idea to keep moving the stop sell order up below the price. Remember to cancel the old stop sell order with your broker. Be careful to put the stop sell order far enough below the current price, so that you will not get sold out by the normal day to day fluctuations of the price of the stock. It is a good idea to plot the prices (High, Low and Close for the day) of the stock for a while to get a feeling of this. If you want to be super conservative, you can start using the stop sell order as soon as you purchase the stock. This simply provides a protection against loss in addition to the yield.

Chapter XVI

Putting These Ideas to Work

My purpose in this concluding chapter is to identify for you some of the problems and challenges that have arisen for people in the adventure of doing work that they love and of building a prosperity consciousness, as well as to point out how you may apply the principles in this book to overcome them. Solving your money problems will not mark an end to all of your problems, even if you are a person who has wrestled with financial problems your whole life. In one sense, life is problems. The real question is whether your problems prove that there is something wrong with you or whether you regard them as opportunities for improvement. I have been practicing the principles in this book for over a decade now and I can tell you that I have problems—lots of them. They are not the same problems that I had last year, because those have been solved and I now have new opportunities for improvement. This book is not for those seeking a get rich quick scheme. I can tell you that once you make the commitment to serve people with work that you love, your gains will be steady and sure, each one larger than the last and that setbacks will seem to be mere ripples opposing your constant progress. I am very grateful for the benefits that the principles in this book have given me and invite you to have the same.

Some people have their identity attached to their job, saying "I am a manager at XYZ Company" as though the statement were a complete description of their personality. Working at a job provides a sense of loyalty and identity, as well as a ready made group of colleagues. Leaving a job that you no longer want can be like leaving a marriage that you no longer want. It is possible that emotional ties to the job or marriage that have been concealed by your dislike will surface in the form of regret or longing once you have left.

Almost everyone with sufficient courage to start his own business has the idea, "I can do it on my own". If this idea translates into "I have to do it on my own", then you'll find yourself isolated by your independence. In most cases, you will discover that your own business does not come with a ready made group of colleagues. Therefore, it is essential for the independent businessperson to seek and cultivate associations with vendors, customers, competitors and other businesspeople that will provide the interchange of ideas and support formerly provided by colleagues at a job.

Most men have been sold a self-defeating bill of goods regarding financial success. This is the idea that if we have expensive possessions (fine car and fine clothes), then more women will be attracted. This myth works to some extent (as most myths do); however, most men sooner or later discover that a relationship with a woman for whom the possessions are a major attractive factor lacks emotional content and simply serves to re-inforce habits about struggle. Regrettably, some men never discover this.

For women, financial success in a business that you love will make it very clear that you don't need men to provide material goods for you. Although this may sound delightful to female readers, those women who have relied on their helplessness to attract men are likely to feel threatened by the prospect of their own personal financial independence. Additionally, women readers who have used the willingness of their male partner to provide financial support as a measure of judging the loyalty or suitability of a sexual partner will find that new ways of thinking and choosing will have to be developed. This I believe is good news for women, who can select their partners more of the basis of personal preference without regard to finances.

As your income and wealth increase, it is essential that you develop the ability to decline offers to spend, loan or give away the cash that you have in excess of your current requirements. If you have been accustomed to hand-to-mouth finances, then, to a large extent, your desperate financial situation has required that you decline offers to contribute to charity, make loans to even more financially desperate friends and relatives and to waste your money by investing in limited partnerships.

When you have cash in excess to your immediate requirements, your options increase and you can choose to buy the things you want and to provide financial backing to the causes that you support. However, if "I can't afford it" is the only reason that you have had for not spending money, you'll discover that your excess cash will soon be gone with little to show for it.

There are many charities that perform important and valuable service that is worthy of your support. I suggest that you develop the practice of giving away a definite, predetermined percentage of your income to people and causes that you support. There are several benefits to you of this practice of regular giving or tithing (not to mention the benefits to the recipients of your generosity). Benefits to the giver are: The experience of actually HAVING the portion of your income that you do not give away will increase, your need for and your attachment to money will decrease, and you will find out that you can live on less than 100% of your income.

You may choose the recipients of your generosity using your personal values and preferences. I want to add several ideas for you to consider in choosing the recipients. There are people who actually solicit tithes and gifts, by telling potential givers, "If you tithe to me, your income will increase." Claims like this border on fraud, simply because whether or not your income increases from tithing depends on whether you are willing to allow the experience of your generosity to dissolve your attachment to money and has nothing to do with the recipient. Additionally, I suggest that you question the advisability of giving money to people who appear on television with a phone number across the bottom of the screen, whose primary service seems to be appearing on television above the toll free number.

As your income increases, your friends, family and associates may experience envy about your success and covertly, or even openly, disapprove of, criticize or even sabotage your progress toward financial success in work that you love. Do everything possible to enlist the support of these people, keeping in mind that it is a good idea to have compassion for the small minded. It is possible that at some point you'll find their company and counsel far less satisfying than going for your dreams.

POSTSCRIPT

I want to leave you with a word of encouragement. Courage is not fearlessness. Courage is the willingness to move forward fear and all. Discouragement is caused by your fear being stronger than your intention to move forward. There is no requirement that you be without fear before taking action.

A diligent reading of MONEY IS MY FRIEND is likely to activate suppressed psychological material and patterns of body energy suppressed from some event in your personal history. It is a good idea to remember that the past is not only over, but that you survived it.

Come back to this book year after year. The disappointment of failure is brief compared to enduring the hopelessness engendered by the prospect of poverty and never-ending financial worries grinding the life out of you. The promise of free enterprise is being your own boss and taking complete responsibility for your income doing work that you love.

STEP FORWARD AND LIVE YOUR DREAMS

THE VALUE OF SELF-IMPROVEMENT SEMINARS

Thousands of people have already started and grown their own businesses using the principles and techniques in this book. This book contains all the information that you need to start and grow a business that you love. The two and one-half day seminars that I offer will provide you an additional boost, especially in the areas of emotional resolution and creativity development, which require personal instruction. Although I travel extensively conducting seminars, I don't visit every city, even if the course of several years; so it is likely that you will have to travel to attend. I think you'll be glad you did. I look forward to meeting you.

Regular events are:
Money Is My Friend Weekend Seminar
Vivation® Professional Training
Love, Sex and Communication Weekend Seminar
Reclaiming Personal Power Workshop

Write for a current schedule:

Phil Laut
PO Box 8269
Cincinnati, OH 45208 USA

or phone:

1-800-597-1923 or
513-321-4405

Sales Managers and Participants in
Multi-Level Marketing Groups
With a few exceptions, the people in your organization are probably working hard enough to be producing more. You can provide them with copies of Money Is My Friend, so that their efforts are no longer hindered by internal emotional conflicts. Please inquire about our quantity discounts.

Appendix

VIVATION AND THE EMOTIONAL ASPECTS OF YOUR SUCCESS

Since money and financial success are far more emotional issues than most people think, I have included this brief appendix about Vivation, the skill of emotional resolution. Please refer to the order form in the back of the book for information about additional books and tapes concerning Vivation.

Vivation is a skill of emotional integration or resolution. It can be described as a feeling process that involves breathing and that allows you to choose how your feelings affect you. Like most skills, you will improve with practice and probably will require a trained instructor at first, but you can do it with your family or by yourself. Vivation is completely internal and personal, it can be done anywhere, although at first it is usually done lying down in a relaxed position with a Vivation Professional in dedicated sessions lasting 1 to 2 hours.

Vivation is based on the idea that we have a choice about how our feelings affect us. Knowing Vivation enables you to turn this idea into practical reality. Instead of the common alternatives of 1) suppressing, denying or struggling to overcome feelings or 2) acting them out in non-productive ways, Vivation enables you to deal with your feelings in a new way by accepting them as they are. For example, you probably would not want to be the kind of person who feels nothing upon the loss of a loved one; but on the other hands, you probably do not want your well being and effectiveness permanently devastated by the grief resulting from this loss. So, Vivation provides you with a balance; a way to deal with the feelings, that we all have, in a more healthy way.

By learning Vivation you gain the ability to manage what your emotions mean to you, so that the effort to suppress them no longer limits your freedom, happiness and effectiveness. You accept your feelings as they are, can relax and think more clearly. This resolution, produced by the Vivation process, I call Integration. The ability to integrate is a skill that can be easily developed regardless of your age, gender, life situation, or how long any problem has existed.

Although I have personally taught Vivation in my seminars and in individual sessions to tens of thousands of people throughout the

133

world, I can't claim to have seen every human condition. In my personal experience with Vivation and in teaching others, the process can enable you to integrate any kind of suppressed feeling, regardless of cause or how long it may have been suppressed.

As a natural, organic process of your body, integration isn't really something that you do; it is something that you allow to happen. I use boiling an egg as an analogy. To boil an egg, you must bring together the egg itself, sufficient water, a heat resistant container that can hold the egg and the water and sufficient heat to boil the water. Once you have established the proper conditions, additional intervention on your part will not boil the egg faster or better. In fact, pulling the egg out of the water to check its progress will retard the result you intend. Similarly, The Five Elements of Vivation (explained later) enable you to establish the proper conditions in your body for the integration of any feelings.

Integration of any suppressed feeling happens in the present moment, so it is not necessary to regress through your personal history. However, it does not necessarily follow that everything that you have suppressed will be integrated in one Vivation session simply because most of us have suppressed a very large (nevertheless finite) number of feelings. Vivation is like exercise is the sense that it is a challenging, delightful and on-going process. Willingness is the most important ingredient. You can learn to do Vivation on your own in a few short sessions and will find that this ability is worth far more than the few hundred dollars that it may cost you to learn. Having learned the process, you can do it on your own or with someone else.

Like suppression, integration is also FAR less selective than we think. For example, resolution of a childhood incident of rejection often results in an increase in income for businesspeople or a reduction in shyness; resolution of resentment about any authority figure can make it easier to pay your taxes or get along with your boss and resolution of shame from childhood sexual abuse causes sweeping changes in how people relate to members of the opposite sex. Integration has a cumulative, snowball effect in that each integration facilitates the next one.

Integration resulting from Vivation does not necessarily change your emotions, instead you learn to change what they mean to you, how they effect you and your attitude about them. Because attitudes influence behavior, integration produces behavior changes that you'll like.

Emotional resolution offers permanent relief from the emotional problems that can plague your financial life. Some of these are:

134

1. Guilt about asking for what you want.
2. Fear of failure.
3. Fear of envy.
4. Personal insecurity or anxiety of any kind.
5. Procrastination.
6. Fear of loss.
7. Shame about money or about yourself.
8. Any of the emotional inhibitors of success described in Chapters IV or VI.

Many of the people who attend my seminars have used various therapeutic methods to gain insight into the cause and effect of their past. A common statement is, "I know *intellectually* why I behave like I do and I know what I could do to improve, but I just can't seem to change." Analysis can only bring you understanding about yourself; but not necessarily desired changes in behavior. Persistent personal and financial problems are most often caused by unconscious struggle to keep suppressed the emotions that you are unwilling to feel. Since this struggle is unconscious, it is unwise to expect that the rational thinking of your conscious mind alone can produce resolution.

The results of suppressing feelings are: your mind distracts you from the discomfort, in your body armors or tenses to control the discomfort, your breathing becomes inhibited, and an internal conflict is created. Knowing this, you can use any of these results of suppression to free yourself from it. The effectiveness of Vivation comes from the fact that it deals with all four of these results of suppression simultaneously. Skill with the process enables you to establish conditions that result in integration of suppressed feelings in every case.

There are many methods of self-improvement that enable the practitioner to resolve the results of suppression. Psycho-analysis and most forms of meditation resolve the tendency for our mind to be distracted from our problems. Body work (massage, Rolfing) and most forms of yoga resolve the tendency for our bodies to armor or tense up to avoid feeling uncomfortable sensations. Some forms of yoga and breathing exercises of all kinds, including vigorous exercise, resolve the tendency for the breathing mechanism to become inhibited as a result of suppression. Vivation combines the effectiveness of all of these methods, because its use involves the breath, the mind and the body simultaneously.

WHAT VIVATION IS NOT

Vivation is not therapy, regression, religion, psychology, yoga, medicine, hypnosis, anything to join and it is not a substitute for any of these things. You are not required to dress differently, behave differently, act out your emotions in an intensely cathartic way, join a club or anything like that; although you could do any of these, if you wanted to.

LEARNING VIVATION

Learning the Vivation process can be compared to learning to fly an airplane, although learning Vivation is much less dangerous, much less complicated and much less expensive than learning to fly an airplane. At first, you would want an instructor to teach you about the aircraft controls and the characteristics of flight and to provide you with confidence and guidance on your initial flights. After you get the hang of it, you would not want to have to take the instructor along every time you wanted to fly somewhere. To continue the analogy, the challenge of learning to fly a plane involves learning that the airplane flies itself and all you have to do is guide it. The novice pilot tends to over-compensate, flying all over the sky.

Learning Vivation has a similar challenge: that of maintaining awareness of the sensations in your body and balancing the tendency to lose awareness of them with the fear that they will be overwhelming. A big part of learning Vivation is learning THAT you can do it. Vivation is a natural, organic process of the mind and the body. A little practice and some willingness are the primary requirements for learning.

In its application, the Vivation process is 99% about the sensations in your body and produces integration or alignment of the mind and the body to produce results that you want. It is a kinesthetic process, referring to our internal feeling sense. This is not the external feeling sense which enables us to distinguish between wool and silk by touch; but rather is the awareness about our body which, when we raise our arm and close our eyes, lets us know that our arm is raised.

Integrating our feelings is a far faster and more effective method of dealing with problems than only talking about them for several reasons.

1) Kinesthetic processing is faster. Our feelings are far richer and more complete than our thoughts, which are experienced one at a time. Just as a picture is worth a thousand words; it could be said that a feeling is worth a thousand thoughts.

2) Kinesthetic processing is more honest. Your mind can fool you or lie to you about a specific issue for decades, but the feelings about it are harder to deny.

3) Kinesthetic processing allows the process to be self-applied eliminating the requirement for the aid of another person.

Since Vivation is neither mental nor intellectual, it is not necessary to label, analyze nor determine the origin of the feelings that are being resolved. In many cases, insight into your feelings will occur, either during or after the session, but mental awareness is not required for integration.

The Five Elements of Vivation were originated by Jim Leonard in the late 1970's, as a result of his diligent research and experimentation with the Rebirthing process, the then crudely defined forerunner of Vivation. The Five Elements make the process extremely simple and easy for you to learn. These Five Elements are all that is required for you to have emotional resolution. Most people report that they are surprised at the straightforward simplicity of this method. The simplicity in fact is one of the most important advantages. Since the process is natural and organic, it will enhance any other self-improvement methods that you are now using such as exercise, meditation, body work, therapy or yoga. Vivation also works fine as your only self-improvement method.

The Five Elements of Vivation are:
1. Circular Breathing
2. Complete Relaxation
3. Awareness in Detail
4. Integration into Ecstasy
5. Do Whatever You Do - Willingness Is Enough

At first the Five Elements of Vivation may seem to be steps to be used in the order presented. The process will work fine for you, if you think of them that way, although it is more accurate to consider them as ingredients in a recipe where you have to remember to include everything to obtain the result, but the order doesn't matter. The Five Elements work together and each supports the others to cause integration. The function of the first Three Elements is primarily to aid you in getting in touch with the feelings that you have suppressed. Additionally each of the first three Elements is pleasurable in itself. The Fourth Element provides the context shift that is required for integration and the Fifth Element reminds you that Vivation is so personal and so individual that there can be no externally determined way to do it right (or wrong); but rather that your willingness is the essential ingredient.

The Vivation process is completely safe and completely natural. I have personally taught this skill to tens of thousands of people of all ages and in all parts of the world. The Five Elements are the entire methodology involved in the process.

ANSWERS TO THE MOST COMMON QUESTIONS ABOUT VIVATION AND INTEGRATION THAT ARE ASKED AT MY SEMINARS.

CAN I DO VIVATION ON MY OWN? Yes. Most people find that they can learn most quickly and easily with a trained Vivation Professional, who can teach you to do the process on your own in 3-5 sessions. There is no danger in trying it on your own first; however, most people who have tried it on their own before obtaining guided sessions, report that they got only limited results because of the unfamiliarity with the sensations that were activated. Like learning any new skill, practice is required and instruction is beneficial.

HOW LONG DOES A SESSION LAST? There is no prescribed length. Usually individual sessions with a trained Vivation Professional last from 1 1/2 to three hours. Generally after your skill increases, sessions become shorter.

WHAT CHANGES CAN I EXPECT? Since Vivation eliminates suppression you can expect greater relaxation in formerly stress producing situations, reduced tendency to struggle with your feelings, improved sense of humor, freer flowing creativity, elimination of the need to engage in self-destructive patterns, willingness to take action to resolve the situations that you have been putting up with, greater self-confidence.

HOW OFTEN SHOULD I DO VIVATION? There is no standard frequency. One session will serve you. At the beginning, I suggest intervals of 5 to 21 days between sessions. After they have learned, some people like giving themselves daily or weekly sessions. Additionally, with practice you can learn to give yourself a session anywhere anytime.

HOW LONG SHOULD I KEEP DOING VIVATION? Once you learn it, Vivation becomes a life long process that you may use whenever you wish to increase your enjoyment of life and your effectiveness.

IS VIVATION DANGEROUS? No. Vivation is dangerous only to your misery. Vivation consists of the Five Elements as I have described. Clearly, there is no danger in breathing, or in relaxing or in feeling what you are already feeling or in accepting what you are feeling or in being willing to do it your way. The changes that occur in you may be perceived as confusing or upsetting by others who have consciously or unconsciously manipulated you by taking advantage of your desire to suppress certain emotions, especially guilt.

IS VIVATION LIKE _____? This is a common question, where the method of self-improvement that the questioner already either knows about or is using occupies the blank space. I know of nothing that Vivation is like (although many readers undoubtedly notice similarities between the theories that I have presented and other philosophies). I have discovered that Vivation enhances the effect of any other self-improvement method; meditation, yoga, therapy, exercise, religion or any other effective method of self-improvement.

WHERE IS THE BEST PLACE TO DO VIVATION? At first you will make the most progress in a location that is quiet and free of distractions. Once you have increased your skill at tuning in to the sensations in your body, the process can be done anywhere, even while engaged in other activities.

HOW DO I KNOW IF I INTEGRATED SOMETHING? The shift of energy in your body is very evident, although people experience integration differently from each other and differently at different times. Sometimes people feel more alive, sometimes they have a profound sense of relaxation, sometimes they feel stronger, quite often they laugh, and feel peaceful and alert. The experience of integration is most often so evident that if you have doubts about whether you integrated, it is likely that you did not. If any uncomfortable feelings recede slowly into the background of your experience, then it is likely that you chose to re-suppress them. When they shift quickly, then you know you integrated them.

WILL I KNOW WHAT I'VE INTEGRATED? Sometimes you will have conscious insight or memory associated with the sensations that have been resolved for you. On other occasions, it will be a strictly kinesthetic experience without any cognitive insights. The resolution of the sensations is what matters. In some cases you will not know what the session was about until later when you notice how your life is different. Every session will be different, because different suppressed material becomes activated. Additionally, each integration facilitates the next one.

WILL INTEGRATION GIVE ME AN IRRESPONSIBLE ATTITUDE ABOUT THINGS THAT MATTER? No. The resolution of sensations that you had been struggling to avoid frees up a whole lot more energy for devoting yourself to the values and causes that matter to you. Your increased self-reliance and sense of purpose will empower you to create the life that you want.

WILL INTEGRATION CHANGE MY EMOTIONS? No. Nor will it make you less emotional, most people report that they feel their emotions more. Integration changes the way that you relate to your emotions and it changes the negative effect that your emotions have on you, enabling you to consistently use them to your benefit.

IS INTEGRATION PERMANENT? Yes. Making the sensations in your body wrong requires effort and therefore once any particular pattern of sensations is resolved, it becomes natural for the mind and the body to continue to relax about the sensations.

HOW DO I KNOW WHEN MY SESSION IS COMPLETE? You will feel calm, peaceful and alert with no intense sensations remaining. In your early sessions, it is possible to feel somewhat disoriented for a short time (usually caused by unfamiliarity with feeling your feelings so directly and honestly). If you are wishing the session were complete, asking your Vivation Professional if it is complete, or thinking about all of the important things you must do when you get home, then your session is not complete. Keep going.

HOW DO I FIND SOMEONE TO TEACH ME? You can have, without cost or obligation a world-wide directory of Vivation Professionals.

From the US, Canada or the Caribbean phone TOLL FREE

1-800-829-2625

HOW DO I LEARN TO BE A VIVATION PROFESSIONAL? I offer Vivation Professional Training, usually twice per year, once in the US and usually once in Europe, and the people we have trained often train others. There are no pre-requisites for taking the Professional Training. You will learn everything you need to know when you arrive. Being a Vivation Professional is a highly flexible career. Some people work part time at home, some work full time and others travel throughout the world teaching others. Please phone or write for a schedule of events.

About the Author

Phil Laut has been self-employed as a seminar leader, author and publisher since 1976. He wrote *Money Is My Friend* in 1979 and revised and expanded it in 1989. Over 200,000 copies have been sold in ten languages. Before that he graduated from the U.S. Coast Guard Academy in New London, Connecticut and served as an officer in the Coast Guard. He is a combat veteran of the Vietnam War, having served for a year as Commanding Officer of an 82 foot patrol boat during the height of the war there. He is also a graduate of Harvard Business School and worked for six years as a financial controller at a major computer manufacturer.

Regular events are:
Money Is My Friend Weekend Seminar
Vivation® Professional Training
Love, Sex and Communication Weekend Seminar
Reclaiming Personal Power Workshop

For an international schedule of events write to:

Phil Laut
PO Box 8269
Cincinnati, OH 45208 USA

PERSONAL BUSINESS CONSULTATIONS AT REASONABLE RATES

Since 1976, Phil Laut has specialized in helping people earn the income they want from work that they love. Find out whether you may benefit from personal telephone consultations with the author.

You will learn to tailor the unique skills described in *Money Is My Friend* to your own personal desires and financial situation. The call is FREE and there is no obligation.
1-800-597-1923
or 513-321-4405 from outside US and Canada

SUGGESTED READING

Vivation—The Science of Enjoying All of Your Life by Phil Laut and Jim Leonard. Published by Vivation Publishing Co. Complete, most advanced self-improvement book available anywhere. $12.95

Think and Grow Rich by Napoleon Hill. $9.00. Published by Wilshire Book Company, North Hollywood, CA. This is a basic primer on money and worthy of repeated reading. Because it was written in 1937, there is little in it about financial freedom for women.

Secret of Unlimited Prosperity by Catherine Ponder. $5.50 Published by DeVorss & Co., Marina Del Rey, CA. An excellent book about tithing.

The Creative Process in the Individual by Thomas Troward. $12.95. Published by Dodd, Mead & Co., N.Y., N.Y. This is the best book on metaphysics that I have found. Other books by the same author are good, too. (Doré Lectures; Edinburgh Lectures; Bible Mystery & Bible Meaning.)

Your Inner Child of the Past by Hugh Missildine. $4.99. Published by Simon and Schuster, N.Y., N.Y. This is the clearest, most loving psychological book about childhood that I have read.

The Door of Everything by Ruby Nelson. $7.00. Published by DeVorss, Marina del Rey, CA. A wonderful statement of Immortalist Philosophy.

Creative Visualization by Shakti Gawain. $8.75. Published by Whatever Publishing, Mill Valley, CA. A simple and complete description of visualization.

Moneylove by Jerry Gillies. $5.95. Published by Warner Books, New York, N.Y. Particularly good for freeing up your attitudes about money.

The Richest Man in Babylon by George Clason. $6.95. Published by Bantam Books, New York, N.Y. A wonderful primer on the 4 laws of wealth. Written in parables. "A lean purse is easier to cure than to endure."

The Life & Teaching of the Masters of the Far East 5 volumes by Baird Spalding. $7.00 per volume. Published by DeVorss & Co., Marina del Rey, CA. An account of American scientists who visited and lived with immortal masters in the Himalayas around the turn of the century. Full of uplifting ideas.

These books are available from:

The Creative Source
PO Box 11024
Costa Mesa, CA 92627
714-458-7971

Books and Tapes from
VIVATION PUBLISHING CO.

BOOKS

Money Is My Friend by Phil Laut $7.95
ISBN: 0-9610132-2-2
You can make more money doing work that you love. This
100,000 copy bestseller teaches you how to increase your
income, how to budget, save, sell and invest.

Vivation: The Science of Enjoying All of Your Life
by Jim Leonard and Phil Laut $12.95
ISBN: 0-9610132-0-6
Over 50,000 sold. Teaches self-directed skill of emotional
resolution and a wide array of self-improvement methods.

TAPES

Money Is An Intentional Creation of the Mind
with Phil Laut $20.00
Two hour seminar recorded at Unity Church in Minneapolis
covering forgiveness, service, gratitude, certainty and integrity as applied to your financial life.

Principles of Personal Financial Success
with Phil Laut $20.00
Two hour talking work book that offers the listener the
writing processes necessary to organize his purpose in life,
and his goals and plans.

Skill of Happiness Tape #1 Introduction to Vivation
with Jim Leonard,
The Originator of Vivation $10.00
One hour description and experiential introduction to the
Vivation process and its uses.

Skill of Happiness Tape #2 Self Vivation
with Jim Leonard,
The Originator of Vivation $10.00
One hour guided Vivation session.

Available at your favorite bookseller or from:
VIVATION PUBLISHING CO.
PO Box 8269
Cincinnati, OH 45208 USA
Please add $1.00 per item for postage.
Ohio residents, please add 5.5% sales tax.

Vivation Publishing Co.
P.O. Box 8269
Cincinnati, Ohio 45208
USA

In a hurry?
We accept orders on VISA
and Mastercard.
Phone (513) 321-4405

Name (Please print clearly)

Address

City/State/Zip

Total Amount of Order

For Credit Card payments

Card Number

Expiration Date

Signature

ORDER FORM

BOOKS	Quantity	Amount	TAPES	Quantity	Amount
$7.95 Money Is My Friend New, expanded edition			$20.00 Money Is An Intentional Creation of the Mind (two tape set)		
$12.95 Vivation: The Science of Enjoying All of Your Life			$20.00 Principles of Personal Financial Success (two tape set)		

TAPES

$10.00 Introduction to Vivation					
$10.00 Self-Vivation					

SUBTOTAL

(Ohio residents, please add 5.5% sales tax)

Shipping (please add $1.00 per item, shipping free on orders more than $35.00)

GRAND TOTAL

☐ Check here if you wish to receive wholesale ordering information.
☐ Please send me information about your Money Is My Friend Weekend Course.
☐ Please send me information about your Reclaiming Your Personal Power Weekend Course.
☐ I want to become a Vivation Professional. Please phone me about Professional Trainings.
☐ Please send me information about the Vivation Professionals in my area.

M3

BUSINESS REPLY MAIL

FIRST CLASS   PERMIT NO. 17278   CINCINNATI, OH

POSTAGE WILL BE PAID BY ADDRESSEE

Vivation Publishing Co.
P.O. Box 8269
Cincinnati, Ohio 45208
U.S.A.

NO POSTAGE
NECESSARY
IF MAILED
IN THE
UNITED STATES